4 A Perfectly Divine Mess

Bow to your awkwardness. Kneel at the altar of
your failures. Smile at your clumsiness. Befriend your
incompetence. Laugh when you stumble and fall.
These are all perfectly precious waves in the oceanic
vastness of you.

Perfection is unattainable in time, but found
only in presence; the presence of imperfection makes
you real, and relatable, and that's perfect. You'll be
consistent when you're dead. Until then, celebrate
your silly old self, your marvelous inability to
conform, or to live up to any image at all.

Don't bore yourself into a spiritual coma. Say the
wrong thing, just for once. There is such freedom
in allowing yourself to screw up, to be kind to your
mistakes, to kiss the ground as you rise again, to
adore the falling, too.

Don't let your spirituality numb your
humanity, your humility, and most importantly,
your sense of humor.

5 Sometimes . . .

. . . you have to fail to succeed

. . . you have to lose to win

. . . you have to break to mend

. . . you have to be weak to be strong

. . . you have to be wrong to be right

. . . you have to disconnect to reconnect

. . . you have to stop trying to change things
    to change things

. . . you have to say "yes" to saying "no"

. . . you have to cease seeking to truly find

. . . you have to forget to remember

. . . you have to be foolish to be wise

. . . you have to fall to fly

. . . you have to plunge to soar

. . . you have to die to really live!

6 Never Fit In!

Face it. You'll never fit in. And that's a wonderful th_ng.

And there's a very good reason why you'll never fit in. There's no such thing as "fitting in."

You see, objects fit in. *Things* fit in. Lumps of concrete fit in holes. Blocks of wood fit in containers. Humans cannot fit in, unless they have reduced themselves to lumps, numbed themselves to life and adventure and the ever-present possibility of transformation.

Humans relate. Humans feel. Humans experier_ce life firsthand, touch life where life is happening, have attitudes and perspectives that are ever changing, urges that are constantly shifting. Something alive and vital cannot "fit in," no matter how hard it tries. Therein lies the rub—and the freedom.

The secret? Everybody is trying to fit in, and nobody feels like they fit in . . . even when they seem to fit in! Fitting in is not possible when you realize that you are alive and therefore have no fixed self, no constant shape, no "hole" with your name on it.

Because even if you were to fit in, even if they finally let you into the club, at what cost would that come to your mental health, your sanity, your inner peace, your awakening? Would you have to play a role to fit in? Squeeze all that precious aliveness out of yourself? Numb your deepest longings and urges? Behave? Perform? Adapt? Be a good, very kind, or very "spiritual" boy or girl? Say the right thing? Hide what you really feel? Stop asking questions? Try to be something you're not? Deny your true path? Stop exploring? Abandon yourself?

Did you ever really want to fit in, friend? If you were accepted, liked, approved of by others for the role you were playing, the persona you were carefully crafting, the "self" you were holding up, would it truly satisfy? Surrounded by a cast of thousands, playing an empty role devoid of truth, wouldn't you still feel like an outcast, far from home? In the perfect relationship, yet having sacrificed your inner freedom and silenced your precious voice, wouldn't you long to break free again?

It's delicious, ingenious, perfect, intelligent that you never felt like you fit in. It means that you were always alive, and therefore unique and irreplaceable, designed to resist any kind of labeling whatsoever, unable to be pinned down or reduced to a category.

To paraphrase Groucho Marx, you'd never want to belong to a club that would have you as a member.

Friend, I love your rebellious heart.

7 Be the Light

There is a love that cannot die. There is a light that
cannot be extinguished, that time cannot touch.
There is an intimacy so strong and immediate we
spend our lives wondering where it's gone.

Do not seek joy; let it find you, let it creep up on you
in your private moments, unexpected; let it reach
you in the depths of your brokenness and despair
and your exhaustion from seeking it in time.

Love the place where you are, love the ground
upon which you stand, for it is this very ground that
joy is heading toward, the ground from which your
new life will grow, even if now upon the ground, you
find your own inability to wait.

Remain open to the possibilities of Grace, for she
moves in mysterious patterns and cannot be captured
by anyone who tries.

8   Trust in Life!

Don't judge your sorrow too quickly or too harshly.
Honoring the darkness within is not the same as
"wallowing" in it; and cultivating a deep trust in all
of life's weather, including the fog, the snow, the
lightning storms, does not equate to self-indulgence
or a "pity party."

Please understand, your dream of unending
spiritual bliss is beautiful! I love your longing for
perfection! Your fantasies of spiritual enlightenment
are so intelligent. You love the light! And you want to
shine! And inspire others!

But spare a thought for (what you now call)
your imperfections. Find a space in your heart for
the unwanted, the unloved, the rejected aspects of
experience. The homeless man in the street is no less
holy than the pope, no less deserving of kindness.
The rancid dog poop on the pavement is as much a
work of art as the shiny things you seek. There is such
beauty in the deformations and the blemishes,
such creativity in the underworld, such power in the
nighttime. If we refuse to plumb the depths, we are
left only half-alive, however "enlightened" we claim
to be. Artists, musicians, poets, and shamans of all
cultures throughout the ages have understood this.

See your life as an art gallery, friend, a display of
light, color, and every shade. Embrace the full spectrum
of experience, from the grays to the brilliant yellows and

blues, from the sunshine to the storms, from the sacred
to the profane. Hold it all in your prayers, illuminate it
all with the light of loving awareness. Be that awareness!
Dignify all manifestation!

Perhaps your sorrow is here to remind you of the
joy that is about to burst forth. Perhaps the contraction
you feel in your belly is about to give way to glorious
expansion. Perhaps your frustration just wants to
frustrate itself fully and be felt, fully. Perhaps this
moment contains no mistakes! Perhaps the relief you
will feel in time will be infinitely sweeter for your
having suffered so deeply. Perhaps your suffering is
teaching you humility, and gratitude, and quietude, and
compassionate understanding of the pain of others,
and trust—unbreakable trust in life's strange processes.

Don't judge your sadness, your depression, your
feelings of unworthiness so quickly, and don't judge the
sorrows of another, for you really don't know what's
best for anyone, for you really don't know more than
life itself. That which you reject (in another or in
yourself) may actually be much-needed medicine, a
misunderstood teacher, inviting you to a self-love deeper
than you ever thought possible. It may be a threshold
guardian, a gatekeeper of a forgotten kingdom!

And oh, the glory of a life fully felt!

And to your demons, say, "Namaste!"

9   An Unexpected Guru

A "terminal diagnosis" is not the end of your life. It is, perhaps, the end of the life you had hoped for, expected, planned, wanted, or been promised. It is the shattering of your outdated dream of "my life." Your story is going in an unexpected direction; that's all. You are now walking an unexpected and untrodden path. It will take time to adjust, for sure.

Yet perhaps the initial shock hails the beginning of a new life, one that is more authentic, connected, honest, conscious, and saturated with love. However "long" you have left matters little, for this journey to Presence requires no time. Perhaps you are being given an invitation to remember yourself, to focus, to breathe, to root out the unnecessary violence in your relationships and in your heart. You have received a call to shine light on those pockets of suffering you would have never paid attention to before. It is a rude awakening, for sure, and sometimes you may wish to rewind the movie to your life before, or at least fast-forward to the future scene of total healing or remission. That would be nice. But you might miss the grace of the journey, the gifts along the way.

Your life is not ending, only a dream.

True healing goes deeper than the removal of symptoms, deeper even than remission or growth, illness or death. It's the discovery of who you really are, cancer or no cancer at all, infection or no infection, medical intervention or not. It's the remembering of love, connection, the serenity at the core of things, the ground into which you breathe.

You are not, and will never be, a victim, a statistic . . . nor even a survivor. No story can define you, no good story or bad story. You are life, beyond description, perfectly awake to itself in this imperfect human form, and the presence or absence of symptoms is no excuse for forgetting your calling: to teach the world to live, and pass, in peace.

10 The Second Vision

Everything you are looking at,
you have already seen once
through the eyes of love.

In this second vision,
do not judge.

For you do not know
what needs your help here.

And you do not know
what has come to serve you.

Assume there is wisdom in every devastation,
and awakening power in every wound.

And every feeling you push away
may contain medicine.

Gentleness is the only answer.

11   A "Yes" to Life beyond Labels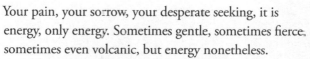

Your pain, your sorrow, your desperate seeking, it is
energy, only energy. Sometimes gentle, sometimes fierce,
sometimes even volcanic, but energy nonetheless.

Strip away the secondhand words and
concepts—*fear, anger, depression, loneliness*—and
contact what is wordlessly alive in your body, not
yesterday, not tomorrow, but *now*.

Feel "sadness" before it is named. Feel the tightness
in the chest, the tension in the throat. Feel "anger"
before it is defined. Feel the burning in the belly, the
pounding of the passionate heart. Feel the throb
and pull of life, the vibration of it. Make space for
all bodily sensations, the raw energy, the power, the
electricity, the sound and the fury. It is life, only life,
always life. Don't judge the energy, or try to push it
away, or ignore it, because then you split yourself into
"good me" and "bad me," "sick me" and "healthy me,"
"spiritual me" and "ignorant me," and the war begins.
Go beyond the entire "me" story, and honor what is
alive in your body, here and now, even if what is alive
is intense, uncomfortable, or simply too unfamiliar to
be named. Let the intensity of bodily sensation focus
you. Let attention drop into the moment.

Non-resistance to life, the absolute surrender
to the living moment, no matter how much the
moment deviates from our "perfect" image—this is
the beginning of true healing.

Divorce the dream and marry reality.

12   Be Exactly What You Are

Don't try to trust; simply trust that you cannot trust
right now or don't know how.

Don't force gratitude; just be grateful that you
aren't grateful, love that the demand for gratitude
is unnecessary.

Love your inability to love fully, accept your
non-acceptance, surrender to your absolute failure
to surrender today.

This is freedom, right where you are—the
freedom to feel unfree, to taste life totally at the point
of creation, to be exactly what you are, no matter
what you are.

Whatever arises, however unwanted, however
disappointing, however ephemeral, say, "You are
none other than life itself! I bow to you!"

13   An Embraceable Mess

You are a complete mess, friend, unable to be
mended.

The time for solutions has passed. Yet stay close.
Breathe. This is not the end. Come out of all your
futures; no time for futures now.

Look: you are an embraceable mess. A mess that
is holy to its very core. You could never be what they
wanted you to be. You were always too alive, too
inquisitive, born with a heart broken open to life.
They tried to close it, but it would never close.

You wouldn't fit in. You couldn't conform.
You could never squeeze yourself into their ideal
of "perfection." The perfect thoughts and feelings,
the "right" way to be, the dance they told you to
dance—your heart was always too big.

Let everything flood in now. Give up. Fall apart.
Break down. Let the old dreams of yourself die a
beautiful death. Let all the lost fragments find safety
in your loving arms.

And in your falling, find yourself. And in your
breaking, breathe.

And all the creatures in all the forgotten
Kingdoms are bowing to you now.

Their savior. Their love.

14   How to Fail Beautifully

Sometimes, even with the best of intentions and hard work, your life doesn't go the way you had hoped or planned or dreamed.

Your heart is broken. Your mind is spinning, confused. You fall to the ground with disappointment, despair. An old feeling of dread comes to visit, a familiar sense of cosmic abandonment. There's a raw, shaky, sinking feeling in the gut, a tightness in the throat, a pressure in the head.

"I screwed up."

In the midst of your hurt, you are tempted to turn against the world, or yourself. Blame someone. Attack someone. Seek revenge, retribution. Or attack yourself, with addictive behavior. Quick, numb the pain. Drink something, eat something, buy something, try not to feel something.

You label yourself "bad" or "wrong" or "broken." You call yourself a "failure," a "waste of space," words you learned when you were young. And then your mind spins off into the future. Not only a day of failure, today, but years of failure to come. A lifetime of failure, ending in death.

You've abandoned the present moment and been pulled into a dualistic narrative of past and future, success and failure, right and wrong, good and bad.

But here is an invitation: *Slow down. Get curious.*

Invite open, curious attention to drop into the present moment. Can you allow yourself to become fascinated with the actual feeling of failure? How do you *know* this is failure? Where in the body do you sense it? Come back to the shaky, raw feeling, the visceral hurt that's alive right now. Come back to the nausea, the heaviness, the pressure, the sinking feeling in the belly. Just for a moment, don't run away or numb yourself from these movements of life. Get curious about the sensations. Give them space; let them dance, move. Don't distract yourself from these precious parts. They simply long for loving attention right now.

You are leaving the heavy story line of "me and my failure." You are showing up for life, connecting with yourself at a moment when you need your own tenderness more than ever.

And out of the rubble of shattered expectations, a new and different life may grow. You may be shaky, broken open, now; your heart may feel tender and raw; your certainties may have crumbled to dust; but you are alive and sensitive, and willing to feel what needs to be felt. And your greatest failure may turn out to be your greatest beginning, the time when you learned more about yourself than ever, the scene of the movie where you discovered humility, courage, and radical self-love.

Stay close; you cannot fail.

PART II   Rest in Not Knowing

15   Stop

Whatever is happening in the circumstances of your life, stop. Just for a moment.

Bring your attention toward the here and now. Let the moment become fascinating. Gently begin to acknowledge what is actually happening where you are. Come out of your conclusions about life, your dreams about past and future, and begin to notice the sensations, feelings, thoughts that are present, right here and right now. Let your present experience—sights and sounds and smells—become the most curious dance in all the universe. You are seeing, tasting, touching, hearing the world as if for the first time. This is your Garden of Eden, your messy, intense, joyous, and heartbreaking Garden of Eden, and you are awake to it at last.

Stop trying to figure everything out. Give in. Give up. Give all to the moment's embrace. Fall into not knowing . . .

16 Unexpected Birds

And sometimes you are walking down a familiar path on a spring morning, and there are questions raging, questions that seem to demand immediate answers. What to do with this precious gift of a life? Where to go? What to say next? Which choice to make or not make? Which voice to listen to? How to make everything okay? How to hold it all together? How to avoid falling apart?

And suddenly the questions cannot hold; they shatter into a million silences because a tiny bird has perched itself on the path in front of you, perched in the *here and now,* not in the *there and then* in which you are seeking your answers. Your eyes meet hers, and you know that everything is okay with the universe. Questions will get answered or not answered, and solutions will appear or not appear at the perfect time, because you will make yourself available to them, as you are available now to this tiny and unexpected bird.

Perhaps today is not a day for answers and unshakable certainties; it is a day for birdsong and staying close to questions as they walk with you down familiar paths on spring mornings.

17 The Perfect Choreography

The mind can only guess at a future.

Be willing to not know, to stumble sometimes, to bow before the unknown.

Stop thinking your way through life, always trying to work it out before living it. Life is to be lived, not analyzed to death.

Feel all the energies that want to be felt, energies that have been waiting so long for your warm attention and embrace. Let all of life move through you, the joy as much as the sorrow, the boredom as much as the bliss.

Let the questions stay awhile; do not try to annihilate them with premature answers. The questions are your intimate friends; the answers are strangers now.

In the warmth of the sun's love, flowers bloom in the perfect moment, and not a moment before.

Let the warmth of awareness illuminate those parts of yourself struggling for life.

See the perfect choreography. Now.

18   Indecision

Friend, please,
do not try to decide now.
Do not shut any possibility out of your heart.
Honor this place of not knowing.

Bow before this bubbling mess of creativity.
Slow down. Breathe.
Sink into wonderment.
Befriend the very place where you stand.
Any decision will make itself, in time.
Any choice will happen when your defenses are down.
Answers will appear only when they are ready.
When the questions have been fully honored and loved.

Do not label this place "indecision."
It is more alive than that.
It is a place where possibilities grow.
It is a place where uncertainty is sacred.
There is courage in staying close.
There is strength in not knowing.
There is power in doubt.

Friend, please know,
there is simply no choice now.
Except to breathe, and breathe again,
and trust this Intelligence beyond mind.

A decision will grow, but for today, nourish the ground.

19   This Moment, Friend, This Moment

Friend, I know that sometimes it feels like everything's falling apart, and even the most beautiful spiritual words sound like meaningless, flowery, new age drivel. We lose everything we thought defined us, or made us happy—everything that seemed to matter to us—and it feels like we will never recover. We are left in total despair, disappointment, disillusionment. It seems like "the end," with no hope of recovery.

Yet in life, there are no true endings, only transformations, new beginnings emerging from rubble. Old dreams die, the false falls away, which can be excruciatingly painful, of course, of course! Destruction, breakdowns, disruptions, shocks, and losses often feel like enemies, but always contain seeds of the new, and sometimes it just takes time to recover. This devastation you are going through, this crucifixion of dreams you feel, is an opportunity to let go of *every single idea* you've ever had of how your life was "supposed to be"—all those cherished dreams that were simply false, yet beautiful and useful at the same time.

The invitation today is to be present to your life, to wake up to it, to turn toward this immediacy, to dignify what is actually happening where you are. If there is loneliness visiting you here and now, do not turn away. If there is fear, do not push it away or try to escape. If there is frustration, anxiety, or just a quiet sense of hopelessness moving in you, do not reject these energies. They just want to be felt, now. They are not wrong. They are your lost children, orphans of awakening, and just want to move and be felt. Sometimes life brings us to our knees so that we will *feel* everything we've been running away from all our lives. And yes, the "meeting" may hurt. But perhaps feeling the hurt is the beginning of healing, not the ending of it.

And watch the mind. How it constantly spins, rewinds, and fast-forwards, constantly leaves the present scene of your life, here and now. Thought is constantly running away from the present moment. It goes into memory—of how good things were before, of how wonderful your life used to be. And it longs to return there. And it feels unable to. And despair results. Regret. Longing. Homesickness. And it fast-forwards into the future, imagining all kinds of scenarios, many dark and scary, some hopeful, but still far. It takes you into regions way beyond your control. And both movements into past and future disconnect you from where you are *now,* which is all there is. They take you away from your only point of power—this moment.

This moment is all there is. This breath. These sensations. Present sounds, smells, tastes, textures. Present beating of the heart, the feeling of your backside on the chair. A little bird singing on the tree outside. The buzz of the television over there. A feeling of contraction in the chest, tenderness in the throat. This is a call to radical, radical simplicity. To honoring the not-knowing. To admitting humility in the face of life. Without the story of past and future, can you really know that your life has "gone wrong"? For that is the belief at the core of everything, isn't it? That your life has "gone wrong." That the "me" has failed somehow. That the universe is cruel and somehow against you. It's an intelligent conclusion to make, yes. I won't judge you for it. But perhaps it's not the truth. Perhaps the mind doesn't know the bigger picture.

My friend, your disillusionment, your inability to believe all those spiritual teachings now, including my own, is not a mistake—it is pure Intelligence at work! Your disillusionment is part of waking up, not the end of waking up! Disillusionment is holy!

You have been given an invitation to a deeper awakening than you ever thought possible. You are being asked now to question everything—everything—including all those cherished spiritual teachings that once held so much value. You are being called to find your own authority, to let go of all those outdated ideas about what life "should" be like. You are being invited to let go of everything secondhand, everything old, everything received—from parents, teachers, gurus, the media—everything in memory, everything in thought, and be present to life, raw and naked.

Sometimes we have to lose everything to remember our humility, that we are not in control, and that each moment is full of wonder and dances in uncertainty. You are on a path of devastation now—it was exactly what Jesus was teaching and living.

This is not the end for you—it is the beginning of a new and different life, a new way of moving in the world, however hard that is to see. It is a time of renewal, of slowing down, of discovering the abundance contained within the nothingness. A time to be kinder to yourself.

There is so much potential for you, friend, even if you do not believe that.

There have been many times in my own life when I felt unable to go on, unable to stand. I felt that I had lost everything, that nothing was possible, that the void was the only way for me. But I just didn't know what the universe had in store. I just didn't know. I was humbled before long.

Even though you feel lonely and abandoned, frightened or angry, friend, know that many others are walking with you, and many others understand. You will write your own book of transformation one day.

This moment, friend. This moment.

20 Beauty in the Breakdown

Oh yes, for sure, there will be heartbreak! And you
will learn to get out of your head and into your
immediate embodied experience, coming out of
mental stories and conclusions, and contacting
the raw energy of the here and now, directly
feeling the devastation of your dreams rather than
intellectualizing everything away, letting the grief,
anger, and sorrow of millennia surge through your
pores, rather than dismissing it all as an "illusion," or
distracting yourself with fresh dreams.

All your preconceived notions of "enlightenment"
will shatter into a million pieces; your happy ideas
of "spiritual awakening" will not survive this, oh no!
You will be forced into a face-to-face encounter with
life, without the comfort of Mummy and Daddy,
without the shield of belief, without the protection of
ego, without the seeming security of fixed reference
points. Even your most beloved spiritual gurus and
philosophers will no longer be of any use.

The raw pleasure and the pain of it, unfiltered, at last! No longer numb, you will be as softly vulnerable as you were in the beginning, before you knew right and wrong, good and bad, God and the devil. At first, this will be terrifying, this total reliance on inner authority, on your gut, on your belly, on your intestines, this absolute openness to experience, this honoring of yourself; but you will learn to trust the path of no path at all, and you will make your nest in the warm bosom of insecurity. And everything will be held in the most profound silence.

Oh yes, for sure, there will be heartbreak! Yet there will be joy, too, the likes of which you've only ever dreamed about!

21 The Way of Rest

Oh, sweet little boy, beloved little girl, you are so overwhelmed by life sometimes, I know, by the enormity of it all, by the vastness of possibilities, by the myriad perspectives available to you. You feel so pressed down sometimes, by all the unresolved questions, by all the information you are supposed to process and hold, by the urgency of things. You are overcome by powerful emotions, trying to control, or at least influence, everything and everyone around you, trying to hold yourself together, trying to make it all "work out" somehow, trying to get everything done "on time," trying to resolve things so fast, even trying not to try at all.

You are exhausted, sweet one, exhausted from all the trying and the not trying, and you are struggling to trust life again. It's all too much for the poor organism, isn't it? You are exhausted; you long to rest. And that is not a failing of yours, nor a horrible mistake, but something wonderful to embrace! For the exhaustion is pure Intelligence, and it says, "Let go, let go! Stop trying so hard! Be present!"

Stop pushing for answers right now. Allow everything to rest right now. Take a sacred pause. Allow questions to remain unanswered, for now. Allow space for yourself to breathe today. Allow everything to fall out of control today. Allow yourself to not be able to hold it all up today. Allow yourself to not know how, to not know at all. Allow the heart to break, if it needs to, and the body to ache, and the soul to wake. Everything is so okay, when you get down to it. So okay, here.

And know you are loved, little one. Know you have always been loved, long before you were named, long before you were even born, long before overwhelm came to show you the way.

22   Slow Down

There is no urgency. Summer does not rush toward autumn. One tiny blade of grass is not trying to grow faster than its neighbor. The planets spin lazily in their orbits. This ancient universe is in no hurry.

But the mind, feeling so divided from the totality, wants answers now, wants solutions today, wants to know so badly. It wants to reach its precious conclusions. And, ultimately, it wants to be in control.

But you are not the mind. Mind is an aspect of the whole, but cannot capture the whole.

So slow down, friend. Take a deep and conscious breath. Trust the place where you are, the place of "no answers yet," the precious place of not knowing. This place is sacred, for it is 100 percent life. It is full of life, saturated with life, dripping with life, drenched with life.

Don't try to rush to the next scene in the movie of "me." Be here, in this scene, Now—the only scene there is.

Now is the place where questions rest, and creative solutions grow.

23   Undoubtable

Do not fear doubt.
Do not see it as a sign of weakness,
     or spiritual failure.

It takes great courage to doubt;
to keep looking
when everything around you
screams certainty;

to remain curious, fascinated
when everyone around you
seems so sure of themselves.

Stay close to your doubt.
It is a gateway to mystery
and the deepest kind of humility.

Your doubt keeps you open and young in spirit,
and ultimately saves you
from the pain of being right,
the shame of being wrong,
and the arrogance of premature conclusions.

Beyond the edges of mind,
beyond the boundaries of right and wrong,
there is this
undoubtable heart.

24　Choice and Miracles

Today, you choose to make or not make a choice.
You decide or don't decide that now is not a time
for decisions. Perhaps today is a time for honoring
uncertainty, holding it close, rendering sacred this
very familiar place of "no answers yet."

There is no choice but to be here, where you
are now, an ancient place where both certainty and
indecision are allowed, both choice and lack of it,
both answers and unanswered questions, and the
most profound doubt. There is no choice because
this moment is already exactly as it is, this breath,
these thoughts, this glorious uncertainty, this vastness
in which everything is possible.

You choose, and you have no choice but to choose.
Or you don't choose, and you have no choice but to
sink into your lack of choice, bow to it, today.

And then the entire notion of choice, and with it,
the notion of the "one who chooses or doesn't choose"
dissolves into sunsets and swallows and the scent
of lavender, and laughter, and the next exhale, and
the next inhale, the breath breathing itself, and this
is the age of miracles.

25   First You Must Ride

Again and again, you will find yourself on that road,
halfway between the life you left behind and the
life you have not yet claimed. And for a moment,
breathless, you will forget the destination, forget
where you are going because your heart is ablaze, and
the wind is in your hair, and the world cannot keep
up with you. You are too fast for this world, too alive
to think about consequences.

You have risked everything to ride on this road,
risked ridicule and rejection and your precious
reputation, but you have chosen life over death,
freedom over approval, speed over stagnation.

You have fallen in love with the unknown again.

The destination will show itself, yes, a new life will
rise, but first you must ride, guided only by some
inner knowing, a little frightened but in awe of your
own courage.

26   The Dizziness of Freedom

The rain's falling on your head, and you brought
no protection. Exposed, raw, you find yourself
taking the next step. The heart breaking open, torn,
ruptured, a bloody mess, only to reveal a thrilling
courage you had forgotten in your search for
comfort, and a kindness that only those who have
suffered will understand.

This strange love affair with uncertainty. The
dizzying vastness of freedom. A tingly aliveness in the
gut that you mistook for pathology. The path leading
only into the unknown, all signposts gone.

Not a path for the faint of heart, no, but for those
who cannot lie any longer. And for those who have
no other choice but to live.

If it makes you weep, if it scares the crap out
of you, if it takes you to the bleeding edge of your
identity and makes you want to vomit . . . well, it
may just be your true path.

PART III

Rest in Pain and Devastation

27   Dealing with Physical Pain

Your pain, the present discomfort in your body, is
nothing to be ashamed of. It is not a sign of your failure,
your brokenness, your weakness, or your stupidity. It
is not a punishment, a test, or even "bad luck." It is
neither meaningless nor the entire meaning of your
life. It does, however, contain great intelligence, if
you know where, and how, to look.

Friend, begin to see that there is a world of
difference between your physical pain, the moment
by moment sensations in your physical body,
happening right now, and your suffering *surrounding*
your pain, your *thoughts about* your pain, your
psychological *resistance* to it. Ask yourself, how much
are you actually connecting with your pain today,
being mindful of it moment by moment, feeling the
raw sensations in the body, and how much are you
thinking *about* your pain, ruminating on it, brooding
over it, anticipating it, or replaying it in your mind?
How much are you present with today's pain, and
how much are you thinking about yesterday's pain,
or lack of pain, or imagining tomorrow's pain, this
evening's pain, or even pain a moment from now,
bracing yourself for impact, as it were? How much
are you in reality, and how much are you in your
thought-created fantasies about the pain never going
away, or imagining that it will eventually become
unbearable, or thinking about all the things you did

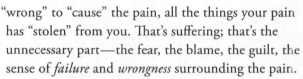

"wrong" to "cause" the pain, all the things your pain has "stolen" from you. That's suffering; that's the unnecessary part—the fear, the blame, the guilt, the sense of *failure* and *wrongness* surrounding the pain.

Pain is simply the body's call for attention; it is not a sign that you, as a person, are broken. Here's an invitation to begin to accept your pain, as it is. Now, let's be clear about this: acceptance does not mean necessarily liking your pain, just aligning with the fact that it is here today. It doesn't mean giving up on the possibility that the pain will lessen or even disappear tomorrow, or next week, or next year. It doesn't mean that you won't find a "cure" for the pain, eventually. *It just means that your peace is no longer dependent on whether or not this happens.* You are reclaiming your happiness, today, no matter what the future brings.

When you resist your pain, fight it mentally, run from it, try to avoid it, distract yourself from it, you become its victim; it has power over you for you are allowing your contentment to be controlled by it. You are giving pain power through your resistance to it, through your focus on trying to get rid of it, trying to escape it, trying to obliterate it, even trying to "heal" it. There is internal violence there. And as you have seen, your attempt to get rid of your pain has failed so far; your resistance has not led to true healing. It has only split you further and further from peace, from gratitude, from love, and from trust in the intelligence and healing power of the body. And it has exhausted you, depleted your energy stores. Think of all the energy that has gone into the failed psychological war on pain—energy that could be used to nourish yourself and truly heal.

Healing begins when you come out of your thought-story that "the pain should have gone by now" (you cannot know that) or "the pain will never go away" (you cannot know that). That is all past-and-future thinking, nightmares and dreams. You stop comparing where you are with where you think you should be, stop focusing on the ever-widening gap between Now and "then." You let go of the story that "I should have lived differently. I created this pain. I am to blame. I am bad. I am guilty. I have failed." That is rewinding the movie of your life, and you have no power in that direction. Remove the burden of time by becoming present to this moment.

So, stop thinking *about* your pain, stop going into the epic Hollywood movie called *Me and My Pain,* and actually commit to *meeting* your pain in the present moment. Bring a gentle, curious, fascinated, receptive, non-resistant awareness to the raw sensations living in your body. For a moment, drop the word *pain* (a very heavy, negative, judgmental word from the past) and directly explore and feel the raw sensations that constitute your present experience. Allow attention to gently move into the physical sensations. Where are they located in the body? Do they feel tight, contracted, tender? Do they have a size, shape, color? Are they moving or still; how are they moving? In what direction, at what speed? Are they heavy, warm, tight, cold, sharp, dull? Drop even these descriptive words now, and bring curious attention to the actual sensations, without labeling them, with a spirit of wonder. Remember, you're not trying to get rid of the sensations, create sensations, or even heal them. (Even the desire to heal can be a form of resistance to the present moment!) You are staying very close, bringing the warmth of your present moment attention to that part of your body that is begging for your love. You are softening around the sensations, making room for them; no longer seeing them essentially as the enemy, but as part of your body; not necessarily likable, but somehow trustable.

Keep exploring. Does your pain have a center? Does it have a boundary? Does it throb, pulsate, vibrate, flutter, sting? Experiment with trying to move your attention to the center of your pain, to see if it has a core. If the sensations begin to move, follow them wherever they go in the body. If they get more intense, that's okay—stay curious. (And if at any point the pain feels unbearable, feel free to stop this exercise, or move attention to a safe place, like the rising and falling movement of the breath, or the feeling of your feet in contact with the ground, until you are ready to explore again. No need to push yourself too hard or fast here.) If the sensations start to dissipate, expand, soften—wonderful, stay close. Don't expect any particular result, but allow any expectations—and disappointments—to come up and be seen, too. Notice if there's any sense of trying to push the pain away, squeeze it out of your body, or brace yourself against it; allow this resistance, too. It's very normal to resist pain or to be afraid of it getting worse; don't punish yourself for this either. Simply notice your resistance and fearful anticipation with an attitude of curiosity and honest inquiry. It's an old habit to see this moment as a threat.

If you wish, you can experiment playfully with the breath. As you breathe in and out, feel or imagine some of your breath flowing into and through the area of pain or discomfort, infusing it with life and oxygen, enveloping the sensations with gentleness, warmth, love. You are dignifying that tender place in you. You are remembering that it has a right to be here, too, a right to be included in the breath and body, not excluded from it. It is very loving to breathe into the pain, not push it away or starve it of attention and air. Instead of contracting around the pain, constricting yourself around it, you are breathing into it, flooding it with tenderness, giving it room, letting it dance its dance. You are honoring the presence of pain Now, rather than demanding its immediate absence. Pain is not happening *to* you—you are the space *for* pain. You cease to be pain's victim when you become curious.

You may begin to notice that pain is not actually something solid, some unchanging lump of *badness* in the body, but an alive amorphous cloud of dancing sensations, changing moment by moment. Pain is *alive*. Sometimes you will look and find that your imagination of pain was much worse than the pain itself. Sometimes you will look and find that the pain is not even there. Sometimes, with kind attention and gentleness, an intense pain will soften, dissipate, relax, become less sharp, more diffuse, warmer. Sometimes the pain may suddenly get more intense, like a wave rising, reach a peak, then fall. Sometimes you will be so absorbed in something else—a piece of music, a conversation, a walk in nature, a meditation, a beautiful daydream—that you will forget you even have pain. (Is pain "there" when you're not aware of it?) Your actual experience of pain is constantly changing, day by day, hour by hour, moment by moment, evolving, shifting, never the same twice. The story "I am always in pain" or "The pain is constant" doesn't even begin to describe the living, moment by moment reality of pain.

Remember, Now is all you are actually facing. Not a lifetime of pain, not even a day of pain, but a moment of it, that's all you are given. The rest is in your mind.

You can see your pain as an enemy, dangerous, essentially "bad" or "wrong," or a "mistake" or "evil," a terrorist or unwanted invader in the body; or you can see it as an ally, even a friend, a meditation bell calling attention home to the physical body and the present moment, which is so often ignored. Many have awakened to the present moment not in spite of pain, but because of pain. Pain—physical or emotional—taught them to slow down, to pay attention to parts of themselves they may have never paid attention to, to come out of stories of past and future, to breathe, and to soften into reality.

Pain can destroy you, or it can focus you. It can drive you deeper into sleep and depression, or it can wake you up. It can turn you into a victim, or it can help you feel more powerful, more aligned, more courageous, more connected with your true path than ever before.

I am not saying that you should try to like your pain. That is unrealistic. I am not saying that you should become a masochist or a fearless warrior and "conquer" your pain. That is unnecessary. I am not even saying that you should give up on looking for a doctor, a healer, a therapist, a helpful friend who can give you another perspective on the origin of your pain. I am asking you—in the meantime, for this moment at least—to listen to your pain, to find the intelligence within. To come out of the heavy, fear-based stories surrounding your pain. To stop thinking about your pain so much, and try a little gentleness, exploration, curiosity. Acceptance, this spirit of *receiving what is,* making room for sensations, thoughts, feelings, can never make your pain worse; it can only lead you more deeply into the vast mystery of healing.

And one day, not so long from now, you may look back and thank your pain for keeping you grounded, curious, open; for keeping you close to yourself, attentive to your precious body, no longer numb to your moment by moment embodied experience of life. You may realize that your pain was not a block to your path—it *was* your path, your greatest teacher.

28 You Are the World's Salvation

Every single day, all over the world, violence beyond comprehension.

How to hold the world's pain in your fragile heart? Ignore it? Deny it? Pass it off as "mere illusion"? Tell yourself, "It's their problem, not mine"? Label others as "evil" and separate yourself from them? Close your heart even more?

Was it not closed hearts and quick judgments that caused this devastation in the first place?

Seeing the daily "realities" of this planet, you may be tempted to give up entirely. Give up on healing, give up on change, give up on humanity itself. What's the point? There's just too much hatred out there. Too much ignorance. Too much evil. We have passed the point of no return, you may say. A fair conclusion. Better to build our walls even higher.

And yet. And yet. Many have suffered the most outrageous injustices and carried on.

Many have carried on, and grown, and healed, and transformed, and brought their transformation to others, and broken down walls.

There are heartbreaking stories of unconditional love shining in even the most impenetrable regions of night.

Focus on what's "wrong" with the world, and you may feel afraid, paralyzed, helpless, full of rage. Focus on what's "right" with the world, and you may just be burying your head in the sand.

Beyond right and wrong, there is a field of indescribable light. Focus on the field.

Focus on the light. Focus on the world that burns in your heart, rather than the temporary reality you see. Acknowledge the reality, yes, but don't use it as an excuse to give up. Use it as an excuse to burn even more brightly, love even more unconditionally, forgive even more radically, question every ounce of evil you have been taught, extinguish every ounce of violence in yourself.

Even a tiny candle can begin to illuminate a vast cavern.

Nothing is "tiny" in the eyes of the universe.

In the Talmud, it is written: "He who saves a single life, saves the world entire."

The world may be broken, yes, but you may be its salvation.

29 The Right Place for Life

Your heart is broken. You no longer feel at home.
The world as you know it is crumbling. You feel you
have lost something very precious to you, something
that defined you, something that made you "you." It
feels like a part of you is missing. Life doesn't seem
fair, kind, right, or even real anymore. You long to
escape, to move away. To rewind to the way things
were or to fast-forward to how things could be. You
feel disconnected, lonely, lost, beyond help. You feel
nobody could possibly understand, for nobody stands
where you stand.

You feel like you are standing in the wrong place,
at the wrong time.

Stop. Breathe. Consider that this is exactly how
things are supposed to be right now. This, this
present scene, is life, not a violation of life.

The universe cannot go "wrong." Life seems to go
"wrong" only in our thinking.

Come out of the movie of past and future,
time and space, and turn to meet a sacred moment,
this moment, the only moment there is. Sense
your own presence, here and now, so still, so
stable amidst the chaos of the world. Feel the
body pulsating, tingling, every part alive. Feel its

heaviness, its weight, the way it is attracted to the ground, pulled downward toward the center of the Earth, giving itself to gravity. Feel the heart pulsing, the belly rising and falling. Feel the raw life that is here, enveloping you, filling you, animating you. Feel the pressure in your head, the fluttery sensations in your belly. Feel your feet on the ground, the way the air moves across your nostrils. Listen to the sounds appearing and disappearing all around you.

Know that the next step can only be taken from here, where you are, the true ground of all grounds. Relax into not knowing what the next step will be before it is actually taken. Trust that you cannot trust right now; the next step will appear in its own time. The true path will emerge; it always does. Be here, Now.

Your heart may be broken, friend, your old dreams may have crumbled to dust, but you're always in the right place for life.

30   Out of the Ashes

Do not despair if you are now feeling far from love.
You are only seeking a reflection of your own heart.
Love is burning even more brightly now, even if it
feels like pain and longing, chaotic sensations in the
belly, chest, throat.

If it is warmth you seek, if it is closeness you
long for, begin by feeling the warmth of your own
broken heart, reconnecting there at the very source
of disconnection, finding presence in your own
presence. Your loved one is near, for *you* are near.

When you feel like seeking outward for love, turn,
come closer, get more intimate with yourself.

Even if you find yourself in ruins now, understand
that even the ruined place contains seeds of grace
and the fragrance of renewal. You cannot go back,
life only marches on. Dignify this ever-onward
movement. The power that was there at the big bang
is still with you; you are undivided from the cosmos.
There is power in your doubt.

Know that a new life can only grow from the
earth upon which you stand. A new painting must
always begin with a canvas. Use the canvas that is
given now. Even old canvases can hold fresh paint.

If you dream of a new tomorrow, your dream appears now, held in your presence. Keep sight of the goal, yes! But never lose connection with the Origin, this moment, the place from which goals are seen or not seen, held or released.

Being present is never in conflict with holding a vision of a more expansive future in your heart, for the holding can only happen in Presence. The present holds the future, too.

And then, out of the ashes of ground zero, that dark place associated only with death and destruction, a new kind of life may suddenly appear possible, and, with love and trust, begin to manifest.

Never give up on life, for it never gives up on you, even when you give up. And know that your heart is near, broken yet radiant. Allow it to be closed now, and it will open when it is ready, and not a moment before.

31 The Beginning of Love

A breakup with a partner or spouse can feel very much like death. Death without actual death, which perhaps is even stranger and more disorienting than death. You feel groundless. You wake up in the morning wondering where they've gone. You look for them and find only their absence radiating, obliterating all the joy of your day. Everything reminds you of them. The way a leaf flutters in the wind. An old tune. A joke you used to share. The remaining, vague shared hope of a happy future.

It feels like you are living in the wrong reality now, like there has been some kind of rupture in the space-time continuum, that the universe has gone off-balance. Their absence is so present in your experience, and the mind longs to go back to the way things were, or at least fast-forward to a future scene when everything will be "right" again.

You watch the mind whirring now, processing, trying to understand, strategizing, wondering where it all went wrong, blaming yourself or them, justifying, denying, resenting . . .

But wait. Perhaps the breaking open of your heart is really the breaking apart of your dreams. And you never wanted to live in dreams. So perhaps, this is your true path coming alive, your path of coming closer to yourself. Perhaps you are being called now to let go of an old reality and meet your loved one in the new reality of the here and now—not as you wanted them to be, but *as they actually are.* To see them, flaws and all, blood and guts all hanging out. The real them, the real you, after all the fantasies have exploded. Maybe life, through the devastation and the heartache and the lost and lonely feeling in the pit of the stomach that won't go away, is making way for a more loving and truthful connection with yourself, and maybe them.

So breathe through the devastation. Feel your feet on the ground. Trust. Maybe true love can never be lost. Death cannot touch it. Endings cannot make it stop. You loved, and you lost, but can you hold the lostness now in love? Can "the lost one" be held? Can you love your grief, your doubts, even your anger, love them as if they were your precious children? And if you can't, can you at least love your own inability to love them right now? Has love truly been lost? Is it not closer than it ever was?

32   The Unexpected Gifts of Pain

"Why am I still hurting? What is wrong with me?"

    Sometimes when you are trying to heal your pain,
or forgive it, or release it, or even "accept" it, what
you are secretly trying to do is *get rid of it*. There is
resistance there to your present experience. You don't
want this moment to be as it is. This moment is your
enemy, your nemesis, even. You want to be someone
or somewhere else: a different body, a different life.
You have split yourself in two: *me* versus *my pain*. You
see the pain as a block to peace and wholeness, or
as some kind of cosmic mistake. It feels like your
entire organism is against you, that you have failed,
that healing is far away, that you are a victim, a
lost cause. Pain is often associated with feelings of
failure, abandonment, shame, despair, *wrongness*.
Uncomfortable sensations in the body often become
unnecessarily entangled with thought-stories in the
mind about a "bad, failed me."

    Please understand this: healing doesn't necessarily
involve the disappearance of pain. No, healing
may involve the pain staying, today. Perhaps even
intensifying. For healing is not a final destination,
but *an ever-present invitation to remember who you
truly are*. It is a call to love, in every moment of
our lives. And in love, your pain is not attacked, or
denied, or pushed away, but given a home. You are
not "in" pain; pain is "in" you, held in the vastness

of your love. It is embraced, even honored for what it is: a powerful expression of life itself, however unwanted or unexpected, however intense or uncomfortable. It is not fundamentally against you, but a frightened part of you that desperately wants to be included, held. It is not a threat, but perhaps your greatest teacher, your most powerful call to presence, to life itself.

This is tough love, for sure. An ancient invitation to let go of all your dreams of how today was going to look, and to honor the way today actually is. An invitation to be vast, vast enough to hold joy as well as pain, heartache as well as bliss, the boredom as well as the excitement of life. And perhaps an invitation to gratitude for the life you have led, for each precious breath, for the food you are given, for the ability to love, to forgive, to connect, to find rest in even the darkest places.

Perhaps your pain holds its own original medicine, its own much-needed teachings of slowness and presence, and taking nothing for granted. Do not rush to label it "negative" and seek to transcend or obliterate it. Here's an invitation to be a little kinder toward it today, however brightly it burns. To not gallop toward its annihilation, but to slow down, get curious, feel its fire, the dignity in its ferocity, its sheer aliveness.

Your pain may be gone tomorrow. That is possible, although we do not want to cling to false hope. We are interested only in truth, Now; pain demands truth, a living truth, the truth of today. So today, we bow before our pain, as long as it is here. We see it as a guest, not a threat.

Presence is the greatest kind of medicine, whatever other kinds of medicine we take or do not take in our search for physical comfort. In Presence, connected to our breathing, feeling our connection with the earth, we cease to be victims, for we are aligned with "what is," on life's side, surrendered to a brilliant and mystifying universe. And that is what true healing is all about. Embracing Now. Saying *yes*.

Your pain just may be what healing actually *feels* like. Your pain may be here to remind you of your courage. Perhaps it's not supposed to have disappeared yet. Perhaps it still has work to do, medicine to offer.

33 Healing: Trust the Process

Sometimes you have to commit to feeling worse in order to feel better. Sometimes you have to lose the hope of ever getting better, then you start to feel better. Sometimes healing involves staying very present as powerful waves of energy move in the body. Sometimes the body shakes, convulses, shivers, aches, sweats, burns, as it rids itself of toxins, releases bound-up tension.

The mind says, "I'm getting worse." The heart knows you're okay.

True healing is not the removal of surface symptoms, but courage, and trust of the body, and connection with the breath, and knowing that symptoms may intensify before they disappear. And they may never disappear. Yet you may fall in love with yourself as you are, despite the future, and you may drop to your knees in gratitude, for you have been given another day on this precious Earth.

Maybe getting worse was the best thing that ever happened to you. Because you've never sensed the presence of love so clearly, and your path has never been more obvious, and you've never felt so alive.

34   Shaking Out the Pain

I was speaking with a woman who'd had terrible
and constant pain in her neck and shoulders for
most of her life. She had been to every doctor; taken
every pill; visited every spiritual teacher; tried every
method, every practice, every mantra. Everything
had only provided temporary relief.

"Why is the pain still here? After all I've done,
with all I know . . ." I've heard this kind of thing
from so many people all over the world. We've tried
everything, been to every healer, had every kind
of spiritual insight and experience, and yet we are
not "over" our pain. It's "still here." We can end up
feeling so disappointed. Like we are failures, far from
healing. Like we are "doing something wrong."

But healing is never far away. I invited the woman
to allow herself to feel the discomfort in her neck
and shoulders more deeply. To be present with
the raw sensations there, moment by moment. To
breathe into them, through them, around them.
To give them space, room to live. To be curious, to
bring them a loving, gentle, receptive, non-resistant
attention. To allow them to intensify if they wanted
to. To allow them to move, to break up, to flutter, to
pulsate, to burn, to spread. But to stay close, to stay
present; to allow, to trust, to breathe.

Suddenly a great terror welled up in her body. An old fear of becoming overwhelmed, of dying, of going mad, of breaking apart. "Allow. Trust. Breathe into this, too," I reminded her. Her entire body started to shake, convulse. "Breathe. Trust. I'm here with you . . ." The convulsions went on for a couple of minutes. I stayed close.

Then the shaking stopped as quickly as it had begun. She opened her eyes. She started to laugh, to cry with relief. "Wow," she said. "Just . . . wow." There were no words. The pain in her neck and shoulders was gone. Her whole body felt rested, relaxed, grounded, warm. She was welling up with love and gratitude.

Instead of trying to "heal" or "get rid of" her pain (she had tried so hard over the years!), she finally was able to meet it instead, make a home for it, allow it, without even the subtle expectation that it would "go away." Her pain had become bound up with emotion—fear, rage, and underneath, great sorrow, even despair. These emotions had been held tightly in her body since she was a little one, when it wasn't safe to allow herself to feel what she felt. So energy had got stuck in her shoulders. Feeling into the "pain" was the invitation for these old energies to finally begin to move in her. Her body was literally shaking out old bound-up energy, in the safety of the present moment, in the safety of our relational field.

She was learning to trust herself again. Trust her body. Trust the power of Presence. Trust someone else to stay close with her in the fire of her experience. Even trust the pain itself, see the intelligence in it. In a space of loving attention, she was able to begin to bear the unbearable, so the unbearable was not unbearable any longer. This is how healing happens—through love, through presence, through the courage to come closer.

35   The Courage to Heal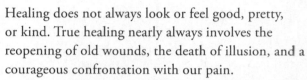

Healing does not always look or feel good, pretty, or kind. True healing nearly always involves the reopening of old wounds, the death of illusion, and a courageous confrontation with our pain.

One of the most unhelpful myths we have inherited from our culture is that healing is supposed to "feel good." No, not always. Sometimes our discomfort actually intensifies as the darkness emerges into the light, as unconscious material makes its way into awareness, as our old illusions burn up. Pain is not wrong, a mistake, or a sign that we are doomed. Pain may actually indicate that our healing process is intensifying, not stalling; that we are actually more awake and sensitive than ever, more deeply connected with the here and now, less willing to look away.

There is such a tendency in our culture to avoid discomfort of any kind, distract ourselves from it, label it as "wrong" or "negative" or even "unspiritual," meditate or medicate it away. Much of our Western medicine is geared toward the removal of symptoms, the silencing of disruption, the numbing of chaos, and the journey toward some socially acceptable sense of "normality."

But sometimes, friend, we no longer have any interest in "returning to normal"! The "normal" was the problem, not the solution! The status quo needed to shift. It was unstable and false. Old dreams were keeping us trapped, limited.

Sometimes our "normality" needs to break open into chaos and crisis; our pain, sorrow, frustration, exhaustion, and doubts need to be felt more fully than ever before; the heart needs to break open more completely.

Our pain is not a punishment from a judgmental god, nor a mistake in a broken universe, nor evidence of our failure and unenlightened ignorance, but a profoundly alive spiritual teaching.

Witness Jesus on the cross. The device of his torture became his ultimate invitation to healing—the rediscovery of his own unbreakable Presence prior to his human incarnation, prior to time itself.

Consider the possibility that within your suffering, you are being given an invitation to let go, to wake up from the dream of normality, to embrace life in all its brokenness and wonder. To fall in love with where you are. To come out of the story of past and future and turn toward the present moment, the place where you stand.

Let the winds blow, let the tempests rage, let all that is false be purified, let all that is dead remain dead, let life explode where you are. You are only being invited to a deeper healing, even though it feels like pain, even though the heart is tender and raw, even though you cannot yet feel your tomorrows.

PART IV   Rest in Melancholy and Loneliness

36 An Exquisite Melancholy,
A Temple of Fire

There is an aloneness that is not loneliness and not despair, and Western medicine is only just beginning to understand. It is something like a profound closeness with your own being, an intimacy with the quiet passing of things, friendship with the broken and the transient within and without.

While you quietly grieve over yesterday's dreams of tomorrows that never came, you hold today so close in your arms. You are the mother of today.

There is a fragility that is not weakness. An exquisite sensitivity to the sad majesty of this ordinary world, a vulnerable openness that has nothing to do with how much money you have made, how you have succeeded or failed in your quest for perfection, or how beautiful or immune to infection your body is, but something to do with the tenderness with which you are willing to touch the broken parts of the world, the depths of aloneness to which you are willing to plunge.

There is an exquisite melancholy that is not depression, contains no pathology, for it contains no self at all. It is as if the heart is broken open and cannot be closed again, ever. Like everything is made of the finest crystal and could shatter at any moment. The sun could burn up without warning, the breath could seize up, a loved one could pass away quietly in your arms. That tiny bird on the tree over there is made of finely woven thread. The neglected pool of water by the supermarket door has infinite depths but no surface, no surface. The moon takes on the quality of a ghost in a dream, and everything is so close. You can touch the horizon, whisper to galaxies.

This melancholy sometimes arrives unexpectedly in the middle of the night, when you cannot sleep, and the moonlight is casting tender shadows on your forearm; or it comes sometimes as you walk through the forest with your dog—you love how he waddles now that he's getting old, your little companion—and you remember what it is like to be free, or at least alive; or it comes unexpectedly at the dinner table with friends, with delight at . . . the salt, yes, delight that the salt could exist at all, that there is a world with salt and food and friends, and the possibility of meeting.

Do not medicate away this melancholy. Go deeper into it. It contains information, important information, and longs to release its healing energies. No, they won't understand you; they will call you depressed, self-indulgent, mad, but you will smile, for you are like the daffodil, and you never wanted to be understood. Your being is too vast to be understood. You will take this imperfect life over no life at all; you will take this broken world blasted through with gratitude over a perfect world half-touched or half-remembered, and the judgments of others will be a small price to pay for never being able to turn away.

Running naked through the streets, throwing off the last of your clothes, you will laugh as they come to lock you up. You are free! You are free! And this beautiful melancholy will keep you from ever closing your heart!

37 Your Other Half Is Within

So many people find themselves searching for a soul mate, their "other half." They feel incomplete, lonely, "single," without that "special someone" in their life.

But you are not half of a whole, friend. You have never been half of a whole. That was the lie. You are whole; that is your nature, whoever comes into, or leaves, your life.

If you are searching for a partner—or staying with a partner—because you feel "half" of a whole, afraid of being alone, unhappy with your delicious solitude, avoidant of the void, you will be bringing your partner into the field of your unhappiness, and anxiety will rumble underneath your days together.

Find your happiness within. Make happiness the field in which you live and have your being.

Discover the joy of your aloneness, the loveliness of your solitude. Enjoy your breath, the way your body moves; feel your feelings, don't wait for anyone to feel them for you. As long as you run away from your aloneness, you will always be lonely, however crowded your life is, because you will be running away from yourself, and that is the greatest pain of all.

Be that "special someone," the one you have always sought. Then, when and if you are ready, allow another dear one into that field. Let them hang out, play, stay if they want, and leave if they want. Take delight in their freedom. Connect deeply. Speak your truth and hear theirs. Notice when you are happy, and notice when you are unhappy, but do not blame them, or credit them, for either.

Help them learn to love their own aloneness, too, to remember that they are also a "special someone" to themselves.

Maybe you will call them your friend, your partner, your lover. Maybe you will marry, maybe you will live together, maybe you will start a family, maybe you will never see each other again. In the joy of deep connection, the labels will not matter so much, and the future will take care of itself.

And you will have found your other half within. And the fear of loneliness will disappear into sunsets, mountains, and the undulating breath.

38   The Gateway of Sorrow

Sometimes it's okay to just feel sad,
without knowing why you're feeling sad,
or how the sadness got there,
or worrying about how long it will stay.

It's okay to feel sad, without trying to not feel sad,
without judging yourself at all.

Feel directly the raw energy in the body, without
    naming it.
Feel the tenderness in the chest, the lump in the
    throat,
the shaky feeling in your belly.
Don't resist the energy, and don't worry about any
    resistance.
Allow the energy to move, to grow bigger if it needs to,
to release itself in its own time.

Be patient with sadness.
Let it come closer, let it engulf you if it must.
Until there is no division between "self" and
    "sadness."
Until you cannot call it "sadness" at all.
Until there is only intimacy.

Be the embrace of sadness, its loving parent,
its home, its protection.

Yes, sadness keeps you soft and flexible.
It reminds you, when you have forgotten,
of the beautiful fragility underneath all things.

In the softness of the heart lies its capacity to love.

Sadness is not the opposite of joy, but her gateway.

The Loneliness of
the Last Dinosaur

Do not fear loneliness, it is not what it seems.
It is your salvation.

Risk everything, friend, risk everything for the love
    of truth.
Let loneliness be the end of "you" as you know
    yourself.
Or at least, let it end the imagination of separation
    from the totality.

You can't tell yourself that you aren't lonely.
You have to die to illusion first to be sure.

Through loss, through break-ups, through illness,
    through the death of dreams, through the passing
    of all that you thought would never pass, you will
    be invited to touch melancholy, meet sorrow in its
    raw state.
And you will be given a great opportunity.
For your loneliness is alive.
Do not build walls around it.
Do not numb yourself.
Do not fall into distraction.
Do not let it solidify into "mine."
Do not become "the lonely one."
What you resist breaks you in two.

Let loneliness breathe. Oxygenate it.
Drop into its depths.
Begin a conversation with it; it is shy.
Do whatever you have to do, or not do, to meet
loneliness without prejudice.

Feel the loneliness of all living beings.
Of Jesus on the cross. The sorrow under the Bodhi tree.
The loneliness of a dying star, of the last dinosaur as
it says good-bye to its broken world.

Feel the exquisite loneliness of this beautiful Earth,
elegantly spinning in the vastness of space.
Feel the loneliness of time itself, never ending, never
beginning, of a universe born of innocence.

Breathe into the big bang, exhale a cosmos.
Die and be reborn.
Reenter the world from a place of intimacy.

Never call it "loneliness" again; the word does not do
it justice.

Can you really be lonely, when every living being
breathes with you?

40   More Alone, Yet More Connected

On this path of awakening, you can sometimes feel
more alone than ever. But this is not an aloneness
that belongs to a separate self. It is not loneliness,
not isolation, not a sense of cosmic abandonment. It
is the aloneness of an entire universe, an exquisite
and intimate aloneness that resides at the burning
core of existence itself. An ontological aloneness
that is perfect solitude, that is the caress of the
autumn breeze on your face, the sound of a little
robin announcing the arrival of the morning, a walk
down unknown paths to destinations unknown.
Nobody and nothing have the power to remove your
aloneness, that's true. You sink deeper and deeper
into this magical place of solitude, touching life for
the first and only time, naked and without protection,
no defenses anymore. Nobody to save you, nobody
who needs to be saved anyway. Past and future are a
billion miles away, and you wonder if anything ever
existed at all prior to *this*. You have found your true
home, at your centerless center.

You feel more alone than ever. Yet, at the very same
time, you feel more connected than ever, closer to every
living being, because you know deep in your bones that
we are all made of the same essence. Your aloneness
does not separate but connects, drawing everything
in, receptive; absorbing the day as it emerges. You are

no longer looking for love and connection because they are already yours in your heart of hearts. You no longer hide from the world because the world is you, and you cannot hide from yourself, and so you can enter so deeply into the heart of relationship. There is no fear of loss of love, and so realness, rather than comfort, security, and fleeting pleasure, becomes the basis of your meetings. You are more alone than ever, yet your relationships are more intimate, deeper, more nourishing . . . and more courageous.

Your aloneness saves you from loneliness. It seems like a paradox for sure, but there is no paradox for you. And don't expect anyone to understand. You have changed so much since they first met you. Simply understand that they cannot understand right now. And love them anyway, as you love the little robin announcing the arrival of the morning, in perfect solitude.

41 The Hidden Invitation of Loneliness

When you're feeling lonely,
it's not the presence of "another person" that
    you're missing,
it's your own warm presence.

In search of another,
you've disconnected from yourself—
and that's the greatest pain of all.

Turn toward the place where you are.
Reconnect with a breath. The morning breeze.
    The sound of the rain. A silent cup of tea.
    Dancing sensations in the belly, the chest,
    the head.

Be here. Sink into gentleness. Watch your
    loneliness dissolve into exquisite solitude
    and a fresh morning.

Be alone, with the miracle of life itself.

42   In Loving Arms

If you feel sad for no reason,
embrace the reasonless spontaneity of your sadness!

In the first light of morning,
when you hear a bird singing her spontaneous song,
you're not pushing for reasons.

Sadness does not arise to be healed.
It arises to be heard.

It arises to be held,
here, Now, in the loving arms of awareness.

43 Room for Sadness?

Your sadness doesn't say, "Please fix me, heal me, or release me." It doesn't say, "Please get rid of me, numb yourself to me, pretend I'm not here." It certainly doesn't say, "Please get enlightened so I can die!"

Sadness does not come to punish you or reveal to you what a "spiritual failure" you are. Sadness is not an impurity or a sign that you are unevolved or far from healing, awakening, enlightenment, peace. The presence of sadness is not an indication that you've done something wrong, that you are damaged or broken, that you are far from the joy you seek.

Sadness only whispers, "May I come in? I am tired, I long for rest."

And you reply, "But sadness, I don't know how to allow you in!"

And sadness replies, "It's okay. You don't need to know. I'm already in. Feel me now, in your belly, your chest, your throat."

And we bow to sadness then; we recognize how it's already allowed in, how there's enough room in us for sadness, how we are not "the sad one," we are not contained within sadness, but we are the room for sadness, its great space, its home, its salvation, its loving embrace; not as a goal, but as our present nature.

Presence is not a destination, so feelings are never a block.

Don't heal yourself from sadness; let sadness heal you. Let it show you the way when you have forgotten. Let it reveal to you the depths of love; let it remind you of your vast heart, your refusal to split off from any part of yourself, your commitment to your body. Let it serve as an invitation to that bigger Happiness you danced when you were young.

PART V   Rest in Discomfort and Discontent

44   All This Shall Pass

Your sadness, your fear, your loneliness, even your despair is so fragile, friend. It can break open at any moment.

A single note in a piece of music can do it. A kind glance from a stranger. The feeling of the spring breeze on your face. The shadow of a bird in flight. In any moment, your sorrow can shatter into nothingness; it has no more reality than that, no more substance than the bird's shadow.

The more you focus on your sorrows and fears, the more you talk about them, analyze them, identify with them, complain about them, resist them, the more "real" they seem, the more solid and independent of you they appear to be, the more power they seem to have over something separate called "you."

In searching for a solution to your problems, you create the problem of "having problems."

Be available for the breaking open of your pain, friend. Do not assume it is here for any longer than a moment. Allow the arrival and passing of all that troubles you, including the very idea of the "me" who is troubled.

All this shall pass, remember, all this shall pass.

45   Stars

You are tired, friend.
Your body aches to rest.

Give in.
You have wanted to fall apart for so long.

To let go of your defenses.
To be transparent and authentic.

Your cynicism has protected you.
Your fear has served you well.

Your dreams of enlightenment were beautiful dreams.
But there is no need to hold your "self" together
    any longer.

Surrender.
Or simply stop pretending that you don't know "how."

Fail.
Fall.
The vastness will hold you.
Only illusions can disappear.

The deeper the heart breaks,
the more love it can hold.

Don't tell me you are not worthy.
Don't tell me you are not made of stars.

46 Get Over It

Don't believe the biggest lie of all: that you're supposed to be "over" something or someone "by now"; that "by now" you should be better, immune, healed, or at least "more enlightened."

If you are "over," then who is "under"? If you are "better," then who is "worse"? If there is a goal, then who hasn't reached it yet? Don't split yourself in two.

Don't attempt to "get over" your grief, your sorrow, your confusion, the empty feeling inside. Feel these friends and allies totally, allow these sacred and misunderstood energies to move through you like tidal waves of grace. They are not "negative," they are only parts of consciousness, fragments of the totality that want to be felt deeply in your vastness. They have come to cleanse and heal, not to punish. Stop naming them or judging them, and start feeling their raw unbridled power.

Don't compare yourself with anyone else. You are unique, awakening in your own original way.

From the perspective of the universe, there is no "by now," there is only Now, and no image of how Now "should" be.

The moment you've photographed a wave in the ocean, it's already vanished.

47 The End of Blame

Your feelings, the energies alive in your body right now, were not "caused" by anyone else, and nobody else can take them away. Now that you are grown, nobody else is responsible for your feelings. This realization can end the blame game once and for all, and leave you standing in your true place of power—the present moment.

Yes, others may trigger pain and sorrow that was latent in you, but they cannot *make* you feel how you feel. They cannot create feelings in you, and they certainly cannot metabolize your feelings for you. Your responsibility lies in how you respond to uncomfortable thoughts and feelings—the kind of relationship you have with them. Nobody can *make* you happy; nobody can *make* you unhappy. You are only invited, constantly, to meet what remains unmet in yourself, to touch what you never wanted to touch in yourself.

Making others responsible for how we feel is the beginning of all violence, both internal and external, all conflict between people, and ultimately all wars between nations.

Let others off the hook. Honor what is alive
in you right now. Learn to hold your own feelings
like beloved children, however intensely they burn
and scream for attention. Celebrate the aliveness in
your hurt, the vibrancy of your disappointment, the
electricity of your sadness. Kneel before the power in
your anger; honor its fiery creativity.

From this place of deep acceptance, you do not
become weak and passive. Quite the opposite. You
simply enter the world from a place of non-violence,
and therefore immense creative power, and you are
open to the possibility of deep listening, honest
dialogue, and unexpected change.

In suffering, you become small. In love, anything
is possible.

48   **The Deal**

The more intensely you feel the joy of life,
the more intensely you will feel the sorrow.
That is the deal.

If you want only half of life,
if you desire light without darkness,
pleasure without pain,
non-duality without the play of duality,
you may wish to turn back now.
(The door will always be open to you, friend.
Come back when you are tired of waiting.)

But if you are ready to live without a reference point,
if you are ready to die to all you think you know,
if you suspect that you are bigger than you were
    ever taught,
if you want to taste all of yourself,
the sorrow as much as the joy,
the pain as much as the pleasure,
then you've come to the right place.

And your entire life
with all its ups and its downs
with all its highs and its lows
has been the perfect preparation.

49 The Gifts of Disappointment

Disappointment can be your greatest teacher
and friend.

You have known disappointment throughout
your life; it has come in various forms, both subtle
and shocking. It has ranged from the gentlest "Oh
well . . ." to the most crushing heartbreak and despair,
the death of worlds. Sometimes it has come in the
middle of the night when your defenses are down.
Sometimes it comes in daylight.

We can pray, align, dream, meditate, and manifest
all we want to. We can attempt to create and control
and contain the perfect life. Yet sometimes, despite
our best efforts, life does not go "according to plan."
The dream is crushed. The fantasy is ruined. A test
result comes out of the blue. A promise is kept or
unkept, broken or unbroken. A plan falls through.
Words are spoken or unspoken. Something you
believed was true was never true. Something is lost
or found, or we discover it never existed at all. And
the ego is humiliated, the seeker threatened, the
self ridiculed. The path is suddenly unclear.
Certainty crumbles.

And the tendency then is to run away from the
sorrow, avoid it, pretend it's not there, make out like
"everything is okay." Or to numb the sorrow with
drink, drugs, sex, gambling, shopping. But the pain
of disappointment is not a mistake, not a block, and

it will open you up, if you let it. It will keep you soft, flexible, and most of all, humble.

The truth is, you don't know. You never knew. And you were never really in control. And sinking into that not-knowing, rather than fighting it, can be the greatest liberation. Humiliation is only a breath away from humility, you see, and endings are nothing less than disguised beginnings.

Assume there is some intelligence in your disappointment, that it is an invitation to connect more deeply—with yourself, with others, with life. You had a dream that didn't come true, and you need to grieve for that lost future, yes, of course. But in the midst of your grief, turn toward the present. Acknowledge the present pain, yes, but do not cling to it, or give it any more meaning than it needs. Let the disappointment take you out of your head and into your heart, into your living body. Breathe. Be present. Feel your feet on the ground. Stay very close to yourself in this time of change. Feel everything. The raw, shaky feeling in the gut. The tightness in the heart. The tenderness in the throat. The pressure in the head. Everything.

Don't skip to the next step. There may be gifts in this present step.

Know that this crisis is only the death of dreams and nothing more. And life has surprises in store.

Stay curious. Cry, shout, wail, weep, punch a pillow if you must, but stay curious.

If you are willing to meet disappointment head-on, there may be no disappointment at all.

50   When Discomfort Knocks

Just sitting with discomfort, without trying to escape or numb it in any way, without expectation, without a goal in mind, without seeking anything, including some abstract notion of "comfort"—that's the juicy place, the place of creative transformation, the place where newness shines.

For many years, I would just sit with my grief, frustration, anger, fear, pain, loneliness, just resting and breathing in that bubbling, burning mess for hours and hours, without trying to escape or fix my experience, without hope, without a dream, without trying to "accept," without time itself . . . until peace was discovered even in the midst of that storm, the unshakable, non-conceptual, ever-present peace that I am, and have always been, the open sky that holds the tumult.

Instead of trying to escape discomfort, we let discomfort reveal its deeper secrets. We sit with discomfort and watch all boundaries between "me" and "my discomfort" melt away, until it is no longer "me sitting with my discomfort" at all, and never was—there is only unspeakable embrace. We sit with frustration in the place where it has not yet coagulated into "I am frustrated." We sit with fear prior to the resurrection of the image "I am the one who is afraid." We sit with anger before the birth of our identity as "the angry one." We know ourselves as the vast open space, the boundless and identity-less ocean that welcomes all of these waves, these raw, alive sensations and thoughts, as its beloved children, returned home at last, home at last.

Discomfort may just be our greatest guru, knocking at the door, calling us to the deeper comfort of Home.

51 The Heart of Suffering

If you find yourself suffering, please pause for a moment, and call into your heart all the people on this planet who are going through similar pain. Remember all your brothers and sisters in heartbreak in all parts of this world. Then think of all the beings in all the universes and throughout the entire cosmos who have known what you are going through right now. Don't see yourself as an isolated entity, or this as an isolated event, devoid of meaning or value, but remember your connection to all there is, to all there has been, to all there ever will be. At the heart of your suffering, know that you are not alone.

Use this moment as an opportunity to connect deeply with compassion—the understanding that nothing is separate from anything else, that we are all on the same basic journey, and that in truth there are no "others" outside of our own hearts. To find compassion for others, you need not leave yourself. To connect with others, simply know yourself more deeply. The journey *in* is the journey *out;* what you love in yourself, you can love in others.

And walk on, connected with your true family, holding them all in your broken-open heart, as you allow yourself to forgive yourself for what you were never able to control.

52   Sacred Exhaustion

Your tiredness has dignity to it! Do not rush to
pathologize it or push it away, for it may contain
great intelligence, even medicine.

You have been on a long journey from the stars,
friend. Bow before your tiredness now; do not fight it
any longer.

There is no shame in admitting that you cannot
go on. Even the courageous need to rest.

For a great journey lies ahead. And you will need
all your resources.

Come, sit by the fire of Presence. Let the body
unwind; drop into the silence here. Forget about
tomorrow, let go of the journey to come, and sink
into this evening's warmth.

Every great adventure is fueled by rest.

Your tiredness is noble, friend, and contains
healing power . . . if you would only listen . .

53   Being with Sensation

Contact a physical sensation without judgment.
Don't think about the sensation, don't analyze it,
    just be with it.
You didn't create it.
You are not responsible for it.
It is not your fault.
You did nothing wrong.
It is not your job to heal it, fix it, get rid of it,
    or even work out "why" it is here.
Like the morning dew or the roar of traffic outside
    your window, it is not personal.
Know less. Feel more.
Commit to the moment.

Come out of the story of past, with its guilt
    and regret.
Come out of the story of future, with its fear
    and anticipation.
Feel the raw sensation now, life in its purest form,
    a dance of energy.
It is here for a moment.
Honor its fleeting appearance.
Be the space for the sensation, its container, its
    presence, its warm embrace.

54   The Breaking Open of Depression

Do you feel depressed?
Then, just for a moment,
feel depressed,
without trying to get rid of that feeling,
without seeking some other experience.

Try taking away the label "depressed,"
and start investigating the aliveness of the body.
Feel directly the raw sensations in your belly,
your chest, your throat, your head.
Do the sensations feel prickly, achy, sharp, round?
Do they pulsate, vibrate, shiver? Are they moving fast
    or slow?
Do they change with attention?
Allow the sensations to dance, to move, intensify
    or dissipate.
Allow all your thoughts, mental pictures, dreams,
    fragments of history, to be here, too.
Allow them to stay, allow them to leave.
Let them be waves in the ocean of You.

Give up the exhausting struggle to change what
    "already is."
Find your rest in the midst of this restlessness.
Pay attention to what is present, not what is absent.
Be the light that illuminates, the kindly awareness
    that celebrates.

Right now, don't try to get rid of depression.
Just listen as the moment sings
its song of constant change.

55   Be Gentle with Anger

Be gentle with anger. Bow before it. It is not what
    you think it is.
Let it come closer, let it enter you if it must.
Feel its power. Until there is no division between
    "self" and "anger." Until you cannot call it "anger"
    at all.
Until there is only fire, passion. But no violence.

Anger is the roar of a lion, the cry of a universe
    longing to be born.
It reminds you, when you have forgotten,
That the power of life moves through you.
That you matter.
That your voice will not be silenced.
That you have self-respect, and deserve to be treated
    with dignity.

Do not push your anger away, or label it "negative,"
    "unspiritual," or even "unhealthy." Do not pretend
    it is not there.
Feel anger's pounding, its vibrations, its fire, its
    longing to be acknowledged, held.
At its burning core, discover your courage.

The courage to be yourself. To hold to your path,
fearlessly. To speak for those without a voice. To
stand up for truth, for your rights, for the rights
of your brothers and sisters, with passion, but
without violence. To roar with love; to let the
world hear your prayers at last.

Know that your heart is vast and spacious, and anger,
so often misunderstood, has a home in you.
Be a sanctuary for lions.

56   A Forgiving Moment

Don't try to forgive yourself, or anyone else, right now. Forgiveness is not a destination, not a "doing," not something you can skip to. First, accept that this moment is exactly the way it is right now. And the past was the way it was.

Accept your non-acceptance in the present. Forgive your inability to forgive right now. Feel your breath, the sensations in your body, the life that burns brightly in you.

Everyone is doing their best, even when it seems like they are doing their worst. Everyone is dreaming or having a nightmare, battling with pain you may never understand. You don't have to condone their actions. You may not be able to wake them up. You don't have to like what happened.

Simply let go of the illusion that it could have been any different. You are different now anyhow. Don't focus on something you have no control over. The past is a distant land.

Bring your attention back to this moment, your source of true power. Your place of connectedness.

Wake up from the dream that anyone has any power to take away your inner peace.

Drop the need to be right. Embrace the need to be free. Come out of the story of "my life." Reclaim the moment.

Forgiveness will come in its own sweet time, and you are forgiven for thinking otherwise.

57 How to Befriend Anxiety

When you feel anxious, don't try *not* to feel anxious, for this feeds the anxiety, adds extra suffering. You end up feeling anxious about feeling anxious.

What you run away from always haunts you. Don't cover up your discomfort or distract yourself from it, or pretend to be "fine" or "okay." Eating, drinking, shopping, pill-popping, incessant talking, whistling, rushing around mindlessly, running to check your messages or contact a friend, trying to control everything around you, spinning off into the narrative of "me and my busy life," these are all ways to avoid the fact of anxiety, ways to abandon yourself in your time of need.

Breathe. Feel your feet on the ground, your belly rising and falling with each breath. Don't think about your anxiety, and how to get rid of it—that is the old paradigm. Feel the anxiety more completely! Can you locate your anxiety in the body—is it in the belly, the chest, the throat, the head? Drop the word "anxiety" (for it is a loaded, secondhand word) and directly feel the living sensations that are there, moment by moment, without trying to get rid of them or stop them, without even hoping they'll go away. Allow yourself to be curious about what's alive in your body right now, about the physical sensations of this moment. Come out of past and future, and dive into Presence. Breathe into the sensations, dignify them with breath, with oxygen, with life, with your kind attention.

Are there butterflies in your stomach? Do your muscles feel tense? Which ones? Can you bring some loving attention and breath there? Let the sensations know that they are allowed to be here, that they are included in life, that you finally have no agenda to destroy them, that they can stay, for now. And there is only Now.

If thoughts are spinning out of control and having a party, if there are many thought-clouds in the sky of awareness, that's wonderful. Don't try to stop thoughts, or silence all these voices, pictures, memories, fantasies, for that makes you more anxious, too. Only thoughts would want to stop thoughts. Be the sky, in which thought-clouds can dance. Thoughts are not reality, not the truth, and not who you really are. They are sounds and pictures only.

Thoughts may be shooting off into the future or past, but that's okay—that's what the mind does: it constantly rewinds and fast-forwards. Yet you are here. You are right here; here is where Presence lives. Allow all thoughts to be here with you, all sounds, all feelings, all urges. Even allow your feelings of non-acceptance, your urge to escape this moment. As the body releases tension, you may find yourself shivering, yawning, laughing, even shaking, or just resting more deeply . . .

If you cannot accept yourself completely as you are, then can you completely accept your complete inability to accept? And if you can't accept that, can you see that even your inability to accept is part of life, part of this moment, part of the movement of the universe? Remember, in truth you don't have to accept yourself, or accept this moment, for it is *already* accepted. It is already here, already alive, already the way it is.

Anxiety is just a little child who has arrived in your space. She has not come to ruin or hurt you, but to wake you up to love. She only wants to be acknowledged, held, allowed into the vastness of the moment.

The anxious one longs for a home in you. Will you run away when she arrives again, distract yourself, numb yourself, or finally turn to greet her, welcome her in, let her know how precious she is?

58 A Path of Radical Inclusion

Everything you push away in yourself pushes back against you: pushing for your love, like a baby in the womb, pushing, pushing, ready to be born, ready to come into the light of consciousness, wanting to be seen. So if you feel something pushing, kicking, aching, a tension, a fear, a doubt, a sorrow, a pain, see it not as a mistake, or an enemy, or a punishment, something "against" your body, a sign that you're far from healing; but see it as your own child, your own flesh and blood, your own body, in fact, an actual movement of you, itself longing for acceptance, love, inclusion, kind attention.

"Include me," every thought and sensation whispers, every joy and every sorrow. "Include me in your vastness, I am worthy. Stop pushing against me, and I will push myself into your loving arms, and you will see, you will know, I am your beloved, I was always your beloved One . . ."

59 Be Gentle with Fear

Be gentle with fear. It is a child of the unknown. It has traveled light-years to find you.

Do not be afraid to feel it fully. It will not harm you. Let it come closer; let it penetrate you if it must.

Feel its aliveness, its pounding heart, its vibrations and tingles in the body. Until there is no division between "self" and "fear." Until you cannot call it "fear" at all. Until there is only life, raw and immediate, and nameless, and benevolent.

Fear is a breaking open into the unknown, a shattering of certainties. It is the forging of a new path into the vastness of night. It is the thrill of being awake.

Fear reminds you that you live on the edge of mystery. That you drink from the fountain of possibility. That your being is vast. That only the false can die.

Do not push your fear away, or label it "negative" or "unspiritual." Do not pretend it is not there. Do not rush to delete it, or transform it, or even heal it. It is not an enemy; it is not a mistake. It is ancient and wise. Bow before it.

Let fear be fear, fully itself. Yet do not be afraid. Let the body shake, let the heart quake. And know that you are present. And opening, and opening.

Let fear, so misunderstood, come to rest in your vast heart. Let it walk with you. When it feels unwanted, hold it close.

Standing on the threshold, you take those first steps into the void.

You are shaking, but you are so damn alive.

60   The Root of Addiction

You can have whatever you want, just not necessarily
in physical form.

The only reason you want what you think you
want, desire what you desire—the cigarette, the
drink, the new car, the promotion, the spiritual
high, the next "hit"—is so you'll feel different, better,
more whole, more complete than you do now. From
a place of incompleteness, you seek completeness in
the world of objects.

What you're really seeking isn't actually the object;
it's the *state* you'll be in when you finally "have" the
object—that sense of release, relief, completeness,
connection to life and love. You'll be able to rest,
finally, your seeking at an end. What you're really
seeking, then, is the *end of seeking,* that sense of being
completely still, and present, and fulfilled, in the
eternal Now.

The root of addiction, then, is this longing for love.
What we truly seek is our own presence. Yet as we all
know, no object, person, substance, or event can
provide you with love. A few moments, minutes,
hours later, the seeking kicks in again. You want
the next "thing," the next hit, the next high, the
next experience, the next "upgraded" moment.
The seeking mechanism was not disabled by the
acquisition of the desired; it simply paused itself
temporarily, then generated more desire.

There is another way. Let desire fall back into its source. All desire is really the desire for Presence itself, the taste of your own being, that cosmic closeness, that gorgeous sense of being alive, awake and open. No object or person can give that to you, although you might get a temporary taste sometimes. But sometimes the taste just makes you hungrier for the meal.

There are many people now on this planet who seem to have "everything," but feel emptier than ever, more lost. The one thing they long for, they cannot find. Presence, stillness, unconditional love, that sense of being home, and deeply rooted in the body, the Earth, the cosmos, however much or little you have—that's the deepest longing of every human heart.

Know that every urge, every longing, every desire, every addictive impulse, is really a call to Presence. Not "future" presence, but Presence, Now! Instead of numbing the desire, or mindlessly following it into a future, habitually reaching out to grab the desired form, get curious; this is the middle way. Breathe into the uncomfortable sensations in the body—the belly, the heart area, the throat—and allow all pictures in the mind, all those imagined "future scenes," scenes of satisfaction and contentment, to arise and fall, too.

There is a deeper contentment that comes from not abandoning yourself now, a more profound satisfaction that comes from staying close to these parts of you crying for kind attention. Not seeking, but staying with the burning, the longing, the urge; listening to what they really want.

From a place of Presence, you are still free to dream, to desire, to imagine goals, to want stuff. Wanting is holy, too; let's not become ascetics. But the quality of wanting is very different now. It emanates from the source, from Presence. It emerges from wholeness, not lack. There is more of a playful attitude now, less urgency, more curiosity. Because now you know, you are whole, whether or not you get the "thing" you thought you wanted.

You are only ever less than a heartbeat away from remembering your own sweet presence, the origin and destination of your deepest desire.

61   You Did Your Best

You did your best. You did all you could do. You had no choice.

Considering what you believed at the time, what feelings were moving through you, how connected you were to your breath, your body, your truth, your path, how rooted you were in the present moment, how clearly you saw or did not see, how much pain you were in, how open and raw your wounds were, how much resistance you felt, how narrow or wide your perspective was, how caught up you were in your personal story, you could not have acted or spoken any differently.

You did your best, given the level of consciousness you were acting from.

Is this an excuse? No. It's about taking full responsibility for what happened, but losing the guilt, "giving up the hope of a better past." Is this a cop-out? No. It's about forgiving yourself. Letting go of "what could or should have been," and aligning with "what is," grounding yourself in the Now, the only place from which true change can happen, new answers can appear, healing can begin.

Grieve over the past, of course. Learn your lessons, of course. Listen to others sharing their pain, of course. Feel everything deeply. Make amends if you can. Say sorry, if it's appropriate.

But do not for one moment think that the past could have been any different. Do not for one moment believe that the universe went wrong. Remove the stories, "I am bad," "I screwed up," "There's something wrong with me."

You are where you are, Now. It is a new day, a new beginning, a new chance to walk your true path.

Armed with new insight, new perspective, a more humble and forgiving heart, a more curious attitude, move into the future, grounded in this loving presence, open to possibility.

How to Be Happy

Don't try to be happy. You'll make yourself unhappy.
You'll compare your present experience with the
mind's secondhand version of "happiness," and you'll
go to war with any unhappiness in yourself, splitting
yourself in two. And you'll feel far from happiness.

True happiness is the absence of trying to
be happy, trying to live up to some outdated,
secondhand image of happiness. It's an invitation to
be whole, grounded, present, right where you are.

Happiness is not a goal then, a destination, a final
resting place. It is a not a state, not even a positive
feeling. It cannot be given, nor can it be taken away.

It is a field. A great field, in which joy and
sorrow, excitement and boredom, loneliness, doubt,
and a profound sense of connection, anger, fear,
uncertainty, even despair are allowed to play, dance,
grow, express, live, stay, rest, and die, in their own
precious time.

All thoughts are welcome, positive *and* negative.
Sounds, both pleasant *and* unpleasant, can come and
go, too.

Happiness is vast; it is not small. It is meditation,
a great space. It is loving attention, slowness, rest. It
is the breath, moving in, moving out. It is the sense
of being alive. It has no opposite, for it embraces all.
It is your nature, not some far-off utopia.

It is you, before you were named, before you learned to doubt yourself.

Don't try to be happy then. Embrace your unhappiness, let it live, offer it asylum and sanctuary.

And you will know a deeper happiness, known as love.

PART VI

Rest in Impermanence and Transformation

63 Changing a Dream World

You have known both joy and sorrow, the greatest ecstasy and the most profound heartbreak. Sometimes the joy was so intense, it broke your heart; and sometimes the despair was so overwhelming, you felt a strange and unexpected joy at its core. Sometimes the joy and the sorrow were indistinguishable from each other, and you were reminded of what lived beyond both—your unshakable presence.

The world has given you so much, friend, more than you ever imagined possible, and you want to give something back. You want to be a force for healing, you want to uplift and create, but so many questions come to visit you in your private moments. How to change the world without opposing it in its current state? How to transform the planet through love and acceptance, not intolerance and war? Must you rage at the status quo, take sides, become an angry missionary, live as an exhausted seeker in perpetual dissatisfaction, in order to bring about creative transformation? Is that the most effective use of your talents? Must you live in fear, anger, and blame?

Great healing begins when *we align with the universe exactly as it is, yet hold in our hearts the way we know it can be, and we simply stop comparing the two.* Keep your eyes on the prize, but do not oppose the present moment—this is the great paradox of transformation, and the secret to changing the world by not changing it at all.

It is impossible for the mind to grasp how creative, intelligent, compassionate, and spontaneous action can emerge from a place of total acceptance of Now; how doing can emerge effortlessly from non-doing.

Acceptance is not tolerance or passivity—it makes you radically alive and passionately engaged with this astonishing dream world.

64   Sing, World, Sing!

Break me open, Life.
Shatter my remaining defenses
against You.

You placed magnificence at the heart of my despair.
You sowed volcanic strength into my vulnerability.
Even my doubt vibrated with courage.

"Leave the familiar
with no hope of return?"
Of course!
I am not afraid. I was never afraid!

I once walked a familiar path of self-construction.
I now walk a path of grace and destruction,
of weeping at birdsong and telling the truth.

I will never turn back!

65 The Beautiful Void Is Rumbling

All your loved ones will die, or change, or leave you—
your mother, your father, your children, your best
friends, your most intimate lovers, your teachers,
your students. Or you will change, or evolve, or
lose your memory, or the body's systems will collapse.
All external sources of happiness are subject to the laws
of impermanence, transience. All forms are ephemeral
in nature; waves in the ocean exist for a moment only,
before changing shape. This is only "depressing" or
"negative" from the point of view of the ego, which
thrives on attachment and possession, and clings to
people and objects and substances for its survival. The
ego always needs time, and makes time into an enemy
or the ultimate addiction.

But from the perspective of who you really are,
the uncontrollability of things, the unpredictability
of others, the beautiful fragility of form, render every
moment infinitely precious. Loss is not an enemy but
a friend, and brings with it an invitation to awaken.

We may not have tomorrow, but we have
Now—and Now is everything.

And so we are pulled forever into gratitude,
broken apart on the altar of fearless love, meeting
in the place where we can never be broken:
Presence itself.

66   Where We Stand

You are lost without hope. Your heart has shattered
into a million tiny pieces today, and you cannot put
the jigsaw puzzle of your life back together, no matter
how hard you try; you no longer have the reference
image. Doubts and questions rage like wildfire
in the vast field of your being. You cannot find a
place of connection anywhere. Even the birdsong
at first light seems to be happening on a remote
planet. Everything that seemed permanent has been
smashed; all your certainties have melted suddenly
into thin air, and nobody seems to have the answers,
not even the gurus and self-help experts who once
promised so much.

    This time, I offer no words of guidance. No
hope, no promises, no dream of this devastation ever
ceasing. You are lost without hope, friend, and what
is left is but a radical commitment to the ground
on which you stand, a marriage of humility to the
Origin, your birthplace, and your final place of rest.

    Sometimes we fall apart, and sometimes in the
midst of falling apart, we remember more clearly
where our feet are rooted. Earth. Ground. Held
by gravity; always falling, yet somehow always
supported. Sometimes we are brought to our knees,
and we remember our knees, and nothing has
happened from the perspective of the ground, save
for the birdsong and the first light of dawn.

67

A Path of Courage and Birdsong

A cancer diagnosis. Loss of livelihood, wealth, image, power. The unexpected end of a relationship. A broken promise, a shattered dream. Impermanence smacks us in the face without much warning. It was always there, of course, lurking in the background; we'd just been distracted, or fallen into illusions of permanence, or become numb.

Impermanence comes, sometimes out of the blue, to remind us of what is essential and true, to shatter our spiritual laziness and remind us of our true path.

A keen awareness of the impermanence of things can protect us from the pain of self-righteousness, arrogance, ignorance, greed—and ultimately, fear itself.

Friend, find that which is permanent in the midst of the ever changing. Find your own presence in the constantly shifting appearances of life. Find your true home in the midst of uncertainty. Be what you are, the unchanging principle—that which has never changed as everything else has changed. Know your own beingness, your original sense of belonging, soft and intimate and warm, always here, never missing. You just got distracted, that's all, became lost in the shiny things, in those intoxicating dreams of past and future, mesmerized by appearances on your way toward future glories promised by undoubtedly well-meaning friends.

And then, a cancer diagnosis. Loss of livelihood, wealth, power. The unexpected end of a relationship. A broken promise, a shattered dream. These are not mistakes or punishments but sudden reminders of the sheer power of the Uncontrollable, the immense Intelligence moving all things, an Intelligence beyond comprehension.

Another call to humility and softness. And kindness. And an invitation to remember: In the midst of cancer, loss, devastation, failure, what cannot be lost? What cannot fail? *Love* is still here. The ability to connect deeply. To listen. To see. To feel. To laugh at seriousness. To be serious about laughter. To remember our own Presence, the Presence of life, here and now. And to bow to the gift of the small things. A sip of water. The sound of the rain. The breath moving across the nostrils. A visit from a loved one. An unspoken kindness. A cup of tea with Father, his hands shaking now. The beauty of questions unanswered.

The essential things cannot be taken away. Everything non-essential will crumble in time.

Perspective is everything. The moment is a beginning.

This is not a path you will find in books, not even this one. This is a path of courage and birdsong, of waking in the morning with a tender heart and knowing that everything is somehow profoundly okay in a way you cannot hope to understand.

68

In and Out of the Now?

We have been taught to think of "the present moment" as an infinitesimally small slice of time, sandwiched in between the past and future, but that is not quite right. Instead of calling it "the present moment" let's call it "the present movement," and see it differently: as the present *dance* of life, this real-time, immediate, vibrant, ever-changing dance of thought, sensation, feeling, sounds, smells, urges, impulses, images, memory, and dreams.

When we take a fresh look at where we are, all we ever find is this present *movement,* not "in" the past or the future, but alive and happening Now. Of course, past and future appear here, too, as images and feelings, as memories and projections. There is only this present movement, inclusive of "your" past and future, and it's all you've ever known, and all you will ever know, for it includes all knowledge and doubt, too.

And then the question is: Who or what is *aware* of this movement? If who you truly are was trapped within this movement, contained within it, defined by it, limited to it, you would never know movement as movement. Simply put, who you truly are never moves and, therefore, is always aware of all the movement of the moment, just as the movie screen allows all movies, all those changing locations and time shifts into past and future, but never itself moves or ages or time travels, always remaining firmly grounded as Presence. You are the silent, still, unchanging backdrop of the present movement of life. All movement happens in, and because of, your presence. You are the one constant here.

The past—as thoughts, memories, images—happens Now, in your presence, not "in the past."

The future—as pictures, plans, hopes, dreams, fantasies—happens Now, in your presence, not "in the future."

Every thought—even a thought about the past—is a present thought. Every feeling—even a seemingly "old" feeling—is part of the present movement of life. Every sound, every smell, every taste, every dream, every desire, happens here, where you are, arising and dissolving in your unchanging Presence, which has never traveled anywhere in time or space.

Now is not a tiny slice of time between past and future, but the capacity for past, present, and future, the unlimited potential for experience, and so we can say this:

You cannot go "in" or "out" of the Now. You are the Now.

69   When a Loved One Passes

When a loved one passes, do not worry. Weep, wail, scream, yes, honor their memory, but do not worry. They haven't gone anywhere, strictly speaking. They have simply lost location and time. You can no longer pin them down, say, "There they are," find them in their materiality, or seek them in your personal world. But you see, they were never tied to their bodies in the first place. Their arms, their legs, their brain, their fingers, their blood, their kidneys, their intestines— these were not the things that defined them. You loved the physical, yes; you were attached to it; you expected it to continue; it was familiar to you; but it was not all of your love.

You are being called now to remember a deeper love, a universal love, a love that is not attached to form, a love that knows no bounds. A love that does not flee into past and future, but remains so very present as you go about your days. A love that does not depend on word nor place, that follows you wherever you go, that is inseparable from your very own presence, that whispers in your ear late at night . . . *"I am here."*

Do not search for your loved one in time or space, friend; do not reach for them; you will find them absent, your hands empty. They are closer than all that. It will take awhile to readjust to their formlessness, of course. You will be called to let go of dreams, yes; and there will be much pain to be felt, much grief to know with courage and willingness. Get ready to break open for love. But, oh, the joy of discovering your loved one right where you left them! And the excitement of a relationship shattering open into the Infinite!

Know they cannot leave you! Know they never will! For they are in your presence, and you in theirs!

70   The Vow of Love

Let us commit to the field of love, not the form.
Let us acknowledge that form changes, ebbs and
    flows, as it must.
We are lovers, we are friends.
We are wedded, we are divorced.
We are together, we are not. We are together again.
We are partners, we are ex-partners. We live together,
    we do not.
We are attracted to each other, the attraction wanes
    then surges unexpectedly.
We are bright and active, rosy faced and full of hope.
We are bed-bound, we soil our underwear at night,
    and we need help to eat, yet we are full of hope.
We take unexpected paths, change in unexpected
    ways, dance our unique dances in the field.
We never stay still. We are alive.
Is there a love that survives all these changes, even
    celebrates them? A love that embraces, yet does
    not cling?
Is there a great field in which we can meet every day,
    in sickness and in health, for richer or for poorer?
Can we commit to the field itself, and not get
    attached to a specific form?

Can we shed all ideas of permanence, and meet in
the here and now, speaking from the heart today,
listening from Presence today, telling our truth
today, no matter where it takes us tomorrow?

Can we risk the loss of form in honor of the field, till
death do us part?
Is there a love so huge, so timeless, so present, so free
from worldly conditions?

71 A Thought from the Paris Metro

Erase the battle lines, my brothers and sisters. Today we begin construction of a new world.

I see a pigeon stuck in a subterranean metro station. Like the human heart, he frantically flaps his wings in an attempt to recover that awesome freedom he must have known before his descent. For now, despite his flapping, the cave remains his tiny kingdom. Yet the bird is magnificent in his flapping, never using his temporary prison as an excuse to give up on his potential, or close himself to the hugeness of his tiny beating heart, the magnificence of each breath.

Sometimes a chaotic reality breaks through into our personal lives. In the external, as in the internal, there are unexpected explosions, sudden ruptures of certainty, traumas—experiences we are unable to hold. Our old conception of normality is torn asunder, and we find ourselves once again in a groundless, unsafe place, uncertain, nothing to hold onto, scrambling to make sense of everything before it is too late, longing for a different moment, a different reality, another chance. Yesterday's insights, joys, enlightenments, revelations, seem a million miles away, like they happened in another life. Perhaps they did. What do we know?

Yet there is only this life. This day. This moment. And in the midst of the storm, we are called once again to remember and not forget our own presence, our ground, the changeless principle amidst this devastating change. And to know the presence of others as our own presence, brilliantly disguised, beyond race, age, religion, even belief. To never be fooled by appearances. Each one believing themselves to be "one" and separate, each one seeking One, each one on their own perilous path toward the sun, flapping in the only way they know how.

Love is like fire. It can burn, but it can also illuminate, and heal, and thaw our frozen fingers, and it kept us alive for all those years before the future came, when we huddled together at night in caves and told stories of loss and courage, and today must have seemed like an impossible utopia.

Utopia. The good place. The place that cannot be, until the disappearance of time.

I am in love with the flapping and with the cracks that humble us and help us remember our shared warmth. You cannot get "there," but keep on trying; love is present even in the flapping of tiny wings.

The Beauty of Good-Byes

Everything ends. Everything, and everyone we love,
is on this Earth for only a short while. We want to
turn from this beautiful fact, try not to think about
it, call the topic "depressing" or "negative" or "too
dark." "Lighten up," we say, desperately attempting
to banish endings—as if they were enemies—from
our lives, burying in mud the pain, the sadness, the
longings, the fears, the dread of eternity, distracting
ourselves with the business of the day, and platitudes,
and "positive thinking," and religions rooted in
fear and secondhand promises, and a refusal to face
Nature and her ancient and mysterious ways. We
struggle to control our lives even more fiercely,
exhaust ourselves in trying to save ourselves from
something from which we cannot be saved.

And still, lurking underneath our frivolity,
our distractions, our attempts to control the
Uncontrollable, the anxiety still rumbles, the ancient
fears of the deep, the specter of loss, the certainty
of the passing of things, often when we least expect
it, or want it, or trust it, or are ready. But as all the
great spiritual teachers throughout the ages have
reminded us, death is a part of the great cycle of life,
and impermanence is built into the very core of our
relative human experience, and nothing is certain
here except uncertainty, nothing is actually promised

except "what is," and we ignore the cycle of rising and falling at our peril.

Everything is burning, as the Buddha taught, and even Christ looked death and decay in the eye, and to a lesser or greater extent, we all must face death in order to value life, to feel fully alive, to know our place in the vastness of the cosmos.

We avoid the contemplation of death really to avoid our own grief, our own heartbreak. But to allow our hearts to break, to soften them, to sink deeply into the knowing that everything will fall, everything will pass, everything will crumble, can be *the* great portal to awakening. We simply stop taking everything for granted. We stop living in "tomorrow" and turn toward the living day. We stop seeking our happiness in the future, clinging to the promises of others, and begin to break open into a bigger happiness that is rooted in presence, and truth, that allows for the coming but also the going of things, that accepts the little deaths as they happen each day, the disappointments, the losses, the shattered expectations, the good-byes. The Unexpected becomes our friend, a constant companion. We break open into bitter-sweetness, into fragility and utter vulnerability, into the gift of every moment, of every encounter with a friend, a lover, a stranger.

Every moment is rendered sacred, holy, because it could be the last one. That is not depressing to the heart, but liberating, nourishing. Because now you are free—free to really live, and love, and laugh, and give yourself fully to existence. Every instant of contact with a partner, a friend, a mother, a father, a beloved child, is seen to be infinite, eternal.

There are no insignificant moments now.

We allow our hearts to break as they open today, taking loss into the bigness of love, holding each other close as we walk our paths, learning to cherish our physicality even though it is burning, ephemeral, ending even as it begins. As Eckhart Tolle reminds us, even the sun will die.

Everything is an illusion, and illusion does not mean "unreal" or "non-existent," but "transient" and "playful," forever passing in our presence, unable to be held for long, and therefore lovable, embraceable, precious, just as it is. Through looking death in the eyes, we discover a happiness that is not dependent on form, and begin to lose our basic fear of living. We find God—the presence of love, light, awareness, eternity—in the midst of our ordinary days, through the gains and the losses, the pleasure and the heartache, the sadness and the most profound joys of this crazy, beautiful human experience.

True love holds within it the contemplation of the loss of the beloved, as every true hello contains its own good-bye, as the sky holds the planets, as the universe holds both the birth *and* the death of distant suns.

"I love you, friend, and I won't always be around in this form, and neither will you, but we are here together, now, and that is everything . . ."

73   The Sacred Heart of Trauma

Sometimes things don't go our way. A loved one
dies. An unexpected test result comes. A relationship
falls apart in a way we never could have foreseen.
An infection returns. A business venture dissolves
overnight. An attack comes out of the blue,
shattering a body or a dream, or both. Something
that seemed so solid and real and trustable yesterday
turns out to be much less than what it seemed. Has a
cosmic promise been broken?

For a moment, all our mind-made defenses
crumble. We are newborns again, no longer
invulnerable, no longer numb to the overwhelming
horrors and glories of creation. We are faced with our
impotence before the vastness of the cosmos, naked
without the protection of ego. For a moment, we
touch and are touched by the unfathomable mystery
underlying and infusing all things.

Sometimes, impermanence bursts through
the gaps in our outdated reality, and the sheer
groundlessness of existence, the uncontrollability
of events, the unpredictability of our emotional
world, becomes obvious once again. Our eyes are
open. Ancient teachings are now alive. What is born
must die. What is here will soon be gone. Ultimately,
nothing is controllable in the external world. The
very ground we stand on can open up at any moment.
There is nowhere truly safe to stand. What is real?

What can be trusted in this life? What is there worth living for?

And we recoil. It's all too much, this hugeness of experience, this *mysterium tremendum*. Quick, get back to normal, to some old safety. Quick, grab on to something solid, something manageable, something tangible. Fix something. Seek something. Control something. Get a grip on something. Get an answer. Medicate. Work it all out. Distract yourself—with substances, with religion, with platitudes, with more and more and more experience.

Switch on the television. Go to the mall. Play a game on your phone. Hide. Hide. Hide.

Rather than face the unexplored terrors lurking in the deep, we fix our eyes once again on the shiny surfaces. We shut out the greater terror of an uncontrollable existence by focusing on the things in life we think we have some control over. We block out our pain and try to get back to normal, back to work, back to the known, back to "reality."

But normality is the problem, not the solution. The old, "normal" reality was too restrictive for us. Life, in its infinite intelligence, was only trying to crack us open. We had become too small for ourselves, too limited, too numb, too preoccupied with seeking self-worth in external things, trapped in our stories, lulled to sleep by comfort and predictability. We had given our power and trust away to external forms and forces. In our pursuit of the positive, we had buried all that we had come to see as negative—the pain, the sorrows, the longings, the fears, the terrors, the awesome paradoxes, the unresolvable doubts. These very natural energies we had pushed into the deep so that we could function, and be productive, and make our parents proud, and be liked, and win awards, and "fit in."

We thought we were happy. Yet our happiness was so contingent, so fragile, and our joy so dependent, and our contentment so very superficial. It was the kind of contentment that could break apart at any moment. And it did, for life seeks wholeness and nothing less.

And we are being called now to question everything. Everything. Perhaps our present disappointment and hurt is not a block to healing but a doorway. Perhaps our grief is not a mistake but a portal. Perhaps even our anger contains a path. And our deepest longings are not faults, but parts of ourselves that just want to be met.

Wounds open to be healed, held, bathed, drenched with loving attention.

Our suffering and the suffering of loved ones can often seem so random, so meaningless, so pointless, so cruel, so uncontrollable, and we rush to cover up our pain, hide it, deny it, or, in our shame, just pretend that we are "over" it. As spiritual seekers, we may pretend that we have gone beyond, or transcended, or even completely annihilated our humanness. That we are invulnerable to the world. That we feel nothing anymore except unending bliss. That we are so very enlightened, so very perfect, so very happy.

But in the end, you cannot hide yourself from yourself, because on some level you always know exactly where you've hidden yourself. The "enlightened me" is the greatest lie of all. Where would the "unenlightened me" hide?

No experience is *inherently* traumatic; no experience is truly unmanageable or unbearable to awareness; but sometimes experiences can release volcanic energies in ourselves that we had repressed, pushed down, refused to integrate in our rush to be a consistent and solid and normal "self." In trying to hold ourselves together, we had actually torn ourselves apart, "good me" versus "bad me."

And now life has come to the rescue with its love of wholeness. The terrors, the rages, the confusion, the unfathomable joys that we were never able to hold, are dancing freely in us again! Hallelujah! The external had to crumble; we are in touch with the internal again!

Here is an invitation to remain raw, uncontained, unresolved a little while longer. Be a little more inconsistent, a little more of a mess today. There is dignity in falling apart, being a little more of your crazy, unhinged, unfiltered, uncensored, uncontrolled self. Bow to all of the ancient energies that are now surging through you. An old life is falling away, a new life has not yet coagulated, and you stand now on holy ground, full of raging aliveness and possibility, broken open but alive to these lost parts of yourself, in touch with ecstasies and pains you thought you would never feel again, energies you had repressed since childhood or even before.

Your suffering is not a mistake, or a punishment, and ultimately, it is not even yours.

We all suffer. We all get ill, get old, and die, at least in our physical forms, and our physical forms are holy, too. We all experience loss, and we all wonder why. We all lose control, or wonder if we ever had control. We are all faced with situations we never would have planned, choices we never wanted to make, things that seem unwanted now, circumstances that just feel "wrong."

But in the midst of the unwanted, if we can slow down, and breathe, and come out of the story of "how it was supposed to be," and come out of conclusions, and turn toward the present moment, we may find things that are okay, even wanted, even sacred, even healing. And we may begin to realize that we are not alone in our struggle. We are connected to all humanity in our hurt. Our suffering is our rite of passage, and many others have been on this journey. Many others have loved and lost, expected and seen those expectations crash. We walk in the footsteps of our ancestors. The ground is always strangely familiar.

We are only being invited to love ourselves even more fiercely, connect with our breath more deeply, feel the kind of compassion for ourselves and each other that we never would have felt if things had continued to "go our way." Whose way, anyway? And why did we expect that things would continue to go our way, in an unpredictable world of impermanence and constant change? Did we really believe that we were in charge? Can a wave control the vastness of the ocean? Did we lose our humility, our sense of proportion?

Everything is dying from the moment it is born, as the Buddha taught. Everything is made of crystal. And therein lies our greatest sorrow and deepest depression, but also our greatest potential for joy and liberation. We learn to get out of our own way, and embrace the way things really are. We learn to love life as it is, and let go of our outdated fantasies. We learn that real joy is not an escape from pain, but the willingness to feel it, and real contentment means opening ourselves up to even the most profound grief. If we can touch our own sorrows, we can touch the sorrows of all humanity. This is not wallowing in our pain, this is waking up, the opening of eyes, the birth of true compassion.

We allow even our deepest pains to remind us of the preciousness of each and every moment of life. We allow life to break our hearts wide open to Truth. Everything is burning, as the Buddha taught, and to cling to outdated pictures of reality only breeds great sorrow.

We knew so much, and now we know less, and that is not a loss, but the birth of our freedom.

And there is something within us that is never traumatized, something ever-present and trustworthy, something unbreakable, something that survives even the most intense sensations, that holds and releases trauma as the heart pumps its blood . . .

74 Son

You are small, but you contain worlds.

You are helpless, yet you shine with the power of life itself. You cannot contain your own power.

When we are together, there is nothing else. You are present, rooted. You remind me of the miracle of being here.

You reach out. You are testing, exploring, carrying out brilliant experiments. You play in a world of desire and thwarted desire, pleasure and pain, sleep and wakefulness. You find your place in between. You take everything in.

You will know sorrow soon enough, perhaps even despair. Great suffering may befall you, yet also great potential for awakening. You may question everything you once believed to be true.

Your path may become unclear. You may stumble in the darkness. I may not be around to help or give answers. That's okay. You will find your own way. Learn to trust your own stumbling. Or maybe your questions will fall into silence, and you will remember the wonder of these days, the ones we spent together before time mattered at all.

You are the illumination, little one, the hope and the possibility. All the darkness in this world seems so insignificant compared to the light and wonder in your big eyes.

I cannot tell if you are old or young. Perhaps the world has it all backward. Perhaps you have lived a thousand years or more. Perhaps this is your final incarnation. Perhaps you have fathered me, so that I may find myself here, next to you, broken but whole, humbled, brought to my knees in gratitude. I do not know. It does not matter anyhow.

I will assume you are ancient and worthy of the greatest love.

And you will remind me of the days when there was strength in being vulnerable, and joy was always near.

75   Ready to Live

Do, or do not. But you will never be ready.

Nobody is ever ready. You'll wait forever to be ready. Readiness is a lie.

You were not ready for birth. Shot out unexpectedly into the maelstrom, you wailed for your life. Terror and overwhelm, breathing, yes, the shock and awe of light, but not ready. And never ready for your first day of school. The fears, the sick feeling in your stomach, a new world opening up, an old world dying, but never ready. And the death of your father, perhaps expected, perhaps prepared for, but not ready. Waves of grief, guilt, maybe, joy, maybe, but how the hell could you be ready? You weren't, but you were alive, and you breathed where he could not, and you took it all into your prehistoric heart. The cancer diagnosis, the loss of your job, that unexpected piece of news. You weren't ready. But you opened. You kept going.

You stumbled, fell, hurt yourself. Picked yourself up. Lost your way. But you were never ready. Ready for what? For a life without pain? For a life without stumbling? For a guidebook? An authority? The answer? You always knew: that was no life at all.

You fell in love with the stumbling, with the doubts, with the mistakes, with saying the wrong thing, with making a mess. You laughed as your dreams crumbled to dust.

Just begin, today, even though you don't know how. Splash the paint everywhere. Cover the canvas with life. Get it all wrong, and feel so right.

You may not be ready, but you are ready to try, to fail, to give yourself to the maelstrom once more.

You may not be ready, so begin.

The Power to Change

Sometimes you reach the end of your tether. You've been fighting to change something for so long.

Now, you realize that it will not change. Not today, anyway. And maybe not tomorrow.

So you begin to accept it, even love it, as it is, now. You bow to its present existence.

Your resistance melts away.

You remember that your inner peace is not dependent on change or lack of change. Your peace is changeless with the seasons.

And then, mysteriously, held in this non-resistant love, feeling no pressure from you to change, cradled in deep acceptance, the thing begins to change.

And you bow to it again.

Sometimes, powerlessness holds great power; the mind is not in charge of change.

77 Held

In my short time on this planet, I have known
great sorrow, plunged into the depths of oceanic
despair, been thrown so deeply into my loneliness
that I thought I would never return. I have tasted
the ecstatic joys of meditation, the fierce intimacy of
love, the savage pains of heartbreak, the excitement
of unexpected success, and the blows of sudden
failure. There were times when I thought I'd never
make it, times when my dreams had been shattered
so thoroughly I couldn't imagine how life could
ever go on. Yet it went on, and sometimes, I found
humility within the devastation; and out of the ashes
of imagined futures, often grew new and present joys,
and no experience was ever wasted.

I have come to trust life completely, trust even
the times when I forget how to trust at all, trust that
life doesn't always go according to plan, because
there is no plan, only life, and even the times of
great uncertainty hold supreme intelligence, and
sometimes you have to fall to stand more fearlessly,
with greater kindness.

And somehow I am always held, in a way I
cannot explain and do not want to. I may be
crushed yet again before too long, I may experience
further seemingly insurmountable challenges
and heartbreaks, but somehow, I am always held.
Somehow, I am always held.

PART VII

Rest in Ordinary Moments

78 These Are the Days

These are the days of our lives. No other days are coming. These are the days.

The days in which we meet each other. Talk or do not talk. Feel what we feel as much as we can feel it. Take the paths we take to the destinations we dreamed about when we could still dream and believe in dreams. Eat when we eat. Sleep when we sleep. Love as much as we can.

But these are the days. The days of ordinariness and miracles. The days of breathing, the days when blood pumps through our veins, the days that seem to last forever, the days that never seem to end. The days where we remain close to life, feel its warmth, its tenderness and its ferocity. The days where anything seems possible. The days where we sit together, drinking jasmine tea, or elderflower, or Earl Grey, or nothing, watching the world go by, ourselves part of the world going by, watching.

Days that make up a life. Days to be lived.

I am in love with these days, given freely. Days to play, to wonder, to seek or not seek, to ask, to remember or forget, but days nonetheless, days whose preciousness is rooted in their own impermanence, whose fragility and solidity seem inseparable.

Do not forget these days, and in particular, this day, the one you inhabit, the one that holds you where you are, as a mother holds her little one, breathless yet robust, pink and tiny and perfect, not without flaws, but loved because of them.

If I am given only one more day, let it be this day, the only day I have ever known, and let me love it the way it has loved me, for all of these days.

79   The Medicine Is Now

Let your present experience become the most
fascinating thing in all the universe.

Whatever is arising in this moment—whether
it's confusion, fear, anger, pain, or just a sense of
not knowing which path to take—let this very
movement be captivating, enthralling; let it fill all
space with its essence. Allow it in completely and
don't judge its existence, whatever it is.

And if you can't allow it in, if there is a struggle
to allow, wonderful! Allow that, too. Allow the
non-allowing. Accept your inability to accept a
single damn thing. Let even that be fascinating, as
it was when you were a little baby, and destinations
mattered less.

Let the whirlpool of this moment become a
stream, and let the stream become a raging river, and
let the river flow into the ocean, and realize that the
very thing you were fighting against was not separate
from that vast intelligence we call Life. It was only
an intelligent cry for complete attention. Water
(consciousness) can take any form—whirlpools, lakes,
canals, rivers, oceans—for it is all there is. Resistance
is futile when you know you are everything.

Nothing to do, nowhere to go. Now is the only
path. The wound contains all the medicine. This is
love beyond the speaking of it.

80 Dare

Today . . .
Dare to allow yourself to be seen.
Dare to tell the truth.
Dare to stop pretending.
Dare to stay present to the secret fire that burns inside.
Dare to be wildly inconsistent.
Dare to let another in.
Dare to let go of the image.
Dare to not be prepared.
Dare to give everything
for the awakening of love.
Dare to fail.
Dare to mess everything up.
Dare to fall to the ground,
humbled again, laughing.
Dare to not know how to dare.
Dare to dream and let dreams die.
Dare to honor the past but not cling to it.
Dare to give an honest "Yes" and an honest "No."
Dare to be wrong.
Dare to be right.
Dare to be real.
Dare to be here.
Today.

81   On Courage

You never knew you had so much courage.

The courage to wake each morning. To take each new breath. To feel each new surge of joy, doubt, frustration, anger, pain, ecstasy, moment by moment, broadcast in real-time, on the aware screen of life. To walk each new step, cross each unexpected threshold, never knowing where it all will lead. To cry when you cry, laugh when you laugh, fall as you fall, rise when you rise. Not necessarily to be unafraid, but to be even unafraid of being afraid.

To think your thoughts, and feel your feelings. That takes great courage.

To begin again, now. To meet each instant with curiosity, fascination, and a little tenderness. To never settle for less than life, less than what it's worth, because it's worth everything, everything that's worth giving.

To greet the day as it plays itself out. To kneel before the dawn. To prostrate yourself before the afternoon and the sparrow singing in your garden. To bow before the evening glow. And then to sink into the embrace of night, and its sleep, and its good death.

And to have the courage to rise again. And breathe again. And dress again. And meet the new day—alive, curious, willing, even though you are raw and without defenses.

You never knew you had so much courage.

82 How to Be Grateful

There is always something to be grateful for. Even
when things go horribly wrong, even when your
dreams die and your plans crumble, even when
loved ones leave and things you never thought
you'd lose are lost, you can always contact a place
of humility, surrender, even awe. And yes, it's not
always easy; and no, this perspective doesn't always
come quickly. But when forgiveness is your path,
and love is your reason for being alive at all, and
awakening is burning in your heart, then gratitude
is never far away.

Gratitude. For connection with a loved one, in the
present. For the air in your lungs. For each precious
breath. For the clothes on your body, however tattered.
For the teeth in your mouth, however rotten. For
the hair on your head, however grey, however wiry,
however thin. For your organs, however infected.
For the liquid you drink, for the food you eat, for the
good earth that provides so much, for the men and
women who toil and sweat to grow and harvest
and transport the ingredients that end up in your
evening meal. For the kindness of a stranger, the
brutal honesty of a friend, the unexpected and
unclaimed gifts of every day.

A part of your body begins to fail, and you appreciate how long it has served you without complaint. Your car is stolen, and you feel gratitude and love for how long you were able to bond with it. You sink into the sweet impermanence of things. A loved one leaves, or passes on, and you appreciate all those moments you spent together, never knowing what the future was going to bring. An encounter with an angry customer shows you your inner strength and your capacity for compassion, and reminds you how deeply people are hurting inside and in need of your kindness. You pay your taxes begrudgingly, unwillingly, then suddenly one day, you appreciate the quality of life you take for granted here, and you burst into song. The skies burst open, and torrential rain "ruins" your day, and out of the blue, there is torrential gratitude for the water that allows life to flourish. You are fired from your job, you mourn, you wail, you scream, and then one morning, it clicks: you are free, free to pursue the thing you always wanted to pursue, the courageous thing, the risky thing, the thing that makes you feel alive, the thing you secretly wanted to do since you were young but always felt ashamed of.

You love and let go. You mourn and celebrate transience. You find your true home in insecurity. You fall in love not with the destination, but with the ground upon which you take each step. You fall in love with the steps themselves. The steps that lead to unknown futures.

Find a place of gratitude today. Find yourself appreciating something for no reason, however small, however silly. Yet know that there is nothing small or silly when seen through the eyes of God.

When you are magical, everything is magical.

83   To Live Is to Die

Living and dying are not polar opposites, but
lovers. To live is to die. To live is to forge ahead with
courage, never knowing where your path is taking
you, sometimes not even knowing if there is a path at
all. To be pathless with courage, courageously pathless.
To live is to risk, to let go of all ideas of what "should"
have been, or "could" have been, or "might" have
been, and fully embrace what is. To be stripped bare
of illusion and to begin again in every moment. To
dream, fantasize, even plan, but, simultaneously,
to let go of those imaginary futures and deeply honor
the living reality, bowing to its awesome power,
prostrating yourself in front of its vastness.

To live is to die to the old dreams, the old ways, to
allow the old fantasies and futures to be destroyed in
Presence, to look deeply into the eyes of Source. To
live is to die to all the images, pictures, dreams of who
you thought you were, or who others thought you
were, and to be what you are, here and now, without
shame. To live is to let go of the story of "me," the
story of past and future and status and achievement
and progress, and courageously open your heart wide
to the living present. To be vulnerable, to trust, to
surrender ego into the vastness of life itself. To be an
ally of the great Unknown.

And to surrender your attempts to surrender, and to let go of your inability to let go, and to accept your non-acceptance. To live is to die to history, and to die to history is to be wide open to Presence as it burns, right now. To no longer be a wave separate from the ocean, to no longer live that illusion, but to be one with the ocean itself; to be an expression of the awesome power that gives birth to suns, grows the grass, and breathes every breath breathed. To die is to be fully alive, to be inseparable from life itself; no longer seeking truth, but being Truth, expressing Truth with every breath.

To die is to be holy, and to live is to be holy. Be holy.

84 Awakening

This is a deathbed, or at least a sanctification. It is an ordinary moment, a seemingly disposable moment, lit up with extraordinary love. It's not some kind of heightened or altered state. States are so fragile; you can drop out of them so easily. Nor is it an achievement of the ego. What the ego will create, life will destroy in time. This is deeper than some passing experience, closer than a thought, more intimate than the most intimate feeling. This is you before you were born, before the universe was even an idea.

You are awake to a new day, and a tiny robin announces the coming of joy and heartache, boredom, and bliss. The first sip of morning tea, and you are complete. If it all ends today, you think, it has been enough, so much more than enough. You laugh until your belly aches, in gratitude, in awe, and offer yourself up in service. A sanctification, a deathbed.

85   The Greatest Gift

Happiness is the absence of the need to be happy.

Peace is not a destination but the absence of the seeker of it.

Love is the death of the hope of a better tomorrow, and the full embrace of today, in its sweet and tender brokenness.

This is the path of the helpless and hopeless, no longer seeking happiness in time, but willing to find grace and gratitude in the most unlikely of places. And to live without hope is a marvelous thing, for it involves wide-open eyes and a being deeply rooted in Presence. And a heart wide open to the gifts of today, forever wandering a path untrodden, revealing its diamonds in the light of awareness. The death of hope is the birth of the new, the emergence of the creative.

Simply take your eyes off the goal, bow your head in reverence to this immediacy, and receive into your arms this living day—the closest thing of all, the greatest gift, the most present present.

86 Reasons to Celebrate

When you are confused, celebrate. In this moment, you're free from having to know, liberated from the burden of expertise. There is no step from confusion to clarity; you clearly see confusion, and so clarity is already closer.

When you have doubts, celebrate. You have remained curious, and you haven't settled for secondhand answers nor fixated on a conclusion. You're free from certainty, the great weapon of the ego, undoubtedly.

When you feel fear, celebrate. You are moving into the unknown, leaving the known world, the dying world, the old world. Stepping into the new. Fear and excitement are so close here. The illusory armor of the separate self is breaking apart; life is flooding in. Fear is trying to protect you; bow to it.

When you feel anger, celebrate. Feel its ferocity, its power, the cry of a velociraptor. Life is surging through you, raw, unfiltered. You are on the verge of finding your song, fighting for a cause with passion, standing up for those without a voice, knowing what you deserve. Anger is related to courage, your willingness to move toward life and protect what you love, even in the face of danger.

When you get lost, celebrate. In every great journey, heroes lose their way sometimes, doubt their own power sometimes. Get lost, and find yourself. Find presence, the breath, the beating of the heart. Take the giant step of not knowing which step to take; a perfect step. Trust the doubting, too. And your path will find you, moment by moment. Your true path cannot be lost, ever.

When you feel sorrow, celebrate. You are not numb. You have not closed your heart to the unwanted. You are wide open to life, sensitive. This old, familiar friend has come to you for help. She is not a mistake. She only wants to warm herself by the fire of your presence, be given a space at the table, next to joy.

When you feel that you cannot celebrate life, celebrate. You are honest, you tell the truth of the moment, your eyes are open.

87   The Sound of Distant Thunder

Give yourself to the first light of dawn, or the crack
in the supermarket wall, or the blackbird laying her
eggs, or the sound of distant thunder. Give yourself
to life in her myriad forms, to every breath, to the
pounding of the heart as it awakens to freedom, to
the majesty of the mountains, to your very own body.
Give all of yourself, and life will give all of herself in
return, for she is a sacred mirror.

Sink into the depths of your aloneness where
the world sings only for you, where, in the place of
loneliness, you find this heartbreaking connection
with all creation. You were born with your heart
open, you were born wide open to life, sensitive to
even the subtlest movements, but you learned to turn
away from your sensitivity. They taught you how to
build a solid self, shut down from the vastness of
experience; to filter your world through thought; to
numb yourself to the gift of feeling.

And it became unbearable to shut off from the
mystery in this way, and through depression, or stress,
or fear, or illness, or a shattered dream or a broken
heart, or sheer exhaustion with the old way, life called
you back to herself and called herself back to you.
Back to the first light of dawn, or the crack in the
supermarket wall, or the blackbird laying her eggs, or
the sound of distant thunder, but now held in your
tender embrace, nourished with your attention.

She did not forget you.

You were never able to work it all out, friend, and that was your victory. You never knew, and that was your innocence, not your pathology. You have remained a child of the universe, eyes wide open, unwilling to conform to anyone's image, unwilling to pretend or settle for anything less than the kind of love that softens stone.

You always had a "Yes" to all of it. Not just the happy stuff, not just the wanted, but the heartbreak, too, and the despair, and the shame, and the doubt. All these were your children, and you their loving parent. And sometimes you stumbled, yes, and sometimes you doubted yourself, and sometimes there was nobody to turn to in your doubting, but you learned to love the stumbling and the doubts, and you learned to trust the times when you couldn't trust, and you found the wanted in the unwanted, and you kept going.

You have been given another day with yourself!

Another day to stay close to yourself as you walk this precious Earth, as you breathe, eat, connect, or do not connect with loved ones or strangers, who are not strangers when it comes to the heart. And it all comes to the heart. And you take the next step, speak the next word, or stay silent for now, and the sun is still the same sun, a day older perhaps, but

constant in its shining, as you remain constant in
your commitment to never abandon yourself again
for another, never turn away from the precious
gift you have been given, the gift of knowing, and
knowing that you do not need to know anything else,
except perhaps the first light of dawn, or the sound
of distant thunder, or the way it feels to be alive, and
ready for love, and willing to fail.

A Teaching Spun of Silk

My words are not meant to be comforting. They are meant to wake you, shake you out of your slumber, shatter your false hopes, your childhood dreams, those secondhand fantasies. And then bring you back, back, kicking and screaming, to the present moment, to that which is alive and well, to this life that burns as Now, to this living Truth, a truth that cannot be taught, only untaught, revealed, forgotten, remembered.

I do not promise piles of gold at the end of the rainbow. I do not offer exalted states and spiritual highs. The highest highs soon turn to lows, and that which is exalted will be derided soon enough. The mind cannot have it both ways. You think you want what you want, but often when you get what you want, it's just not enough. And you want something else. And something else, and more, ad infinitum. And soon you tire of this cycle of unquenchable lack, and this teaching begins to burn.

It gets into your bones. It haunts. It bleeds into every crevice of experience, rendering everything a guru. It is life being lived, not life being reified as clever words and systems. It is waking up in the morning, never knowing what is to come, despite history. It is every precious instant of contact with a friend or loved one, never taking for granted that it could be the last time, the first time. It is the sting of a needle entering a vein. It is the shock of pain surging through the body, calling you to let go of resistance. It is the warmth of the morning sun. It is crushing doubt followed by inexplicable joy, all held in a way you cannot explain or understand. It is walking down an unknown path, feeling disconnected and worn down by the push and pull of things, and suddenly remembering, suddenly recalling life is only a moment, and things are never as bad as they seem because the one place you cannot escape is the one place you long to be. You are delivered from time at last. You taste your own presence again—solid, trustworthy, unchanging despite the changes of another day on this strange and beautiful planet spinning in infinite night.

Back to gratitude and the dawn. And the way the spider spins her web, so fearless despite her fragility, so present to the work of her tiny spinnerets. Liquid silk, and so surrendered to the coming of tomorrows. Everything yet unborn, everything coming into being, everything resolved in its brokenness, everything on fire.

"I love you," you whisper to life. And you spend the rest of your days listening for her infinite replies.

I know no teaching other than this. This, a teaching that lives inside each beat of the heart, shining through every pair of eyes, held in a mother's silence.

89 The Point of No Return

You have to breathe in the stillness. For the world
is fast and ends too soon, and you are so slow and
beautiful in your slowness. The destination is no
destination for you, and never was.

So recontact a moment. Begin where you begin,
here, at the point of emergence. It's not just a cup
of tea, a walk with a friend, words spoken or not
spoken. It's a love affair, the moments flowing into
each other so completely that there are no moments
at all, only the shock and awe of being alive on this
day of all days.

This chance to connect. This ordinariness,
embodied. This unbearable freedom threatening to
crack the earth open. The softening of the heart. The
shadows and the light. The fire and the ashes. I will
give up everything except the horizon, this marvelous
sense of moving forward while staying totally still.

And if I could, I would render it all in the most
delicate glass and show it to this fast world.

PART VIII

Rest in Abundance and Beauty

90 On Abundance

 Abundance is not the money you have in your bank
account, the trophies on your shelf, the letters after
your name, the list of goals reached, the number of
people you know, your perfect, healthy body, your
adoring fans.

Abundance is your connection to each breath,
how sensitive you are to every flicker of sensation
and emotion in the body. It is the delight with which
you savor each unique moment, the joy with which you
greet each new day. It is knowing yourself as presence,
the power that creates and moves worlds. It is your
open heart, how deeply moved you are by love every
day, your willingness to embrace, to hold what
needs to be held. It is the freshness of each morning
unencumbered by memory or false hope.

Abundance is the feeling of the afternoon breeze on your cheeks, the sun warming your face. It is meeting others in the field of honesty and vulnerability, connecting beyond the story, sharing what is alive. It is your rootedness in the present moment, knowing that you are always Home, no matter what happens, no matter what is gained or lost. It is touching life at the point of creation, never looking back, feeling the belly rise and fall, thanking each breath, giving praise to each breath. It is falling to your knees in awe, laughing at the stories they tell about you, sinking more deeply into rest.

Abundance is simplicity. It is kindness. It is you, before every sunrise: fresh, open, and awake.

You are rich, friend! You are rich!

91　From Lack to Abundance

Try to get
what you want,
and it's already
far away.
Be what you want,
know it in your heart,
and it's already yours.
The rest is
details.
The rest,
you never really wanted anyway.
From lack to abundance,
in a heartbeat.

92   How to Have an Abundant Year

What is abundance? Is it about having more money,
more fame, more recognition, more "stuff" than
you really need? Is it about acquiring unnecessary
personal wealth, amassing piles of stuff for yourself
and your inner circle?

No, no, no. It is the raging fire in your heart! It
is the inexplicable joy rumbling in your belly! It is
the heartbreaking gratitude you feel upon waking,
having been given another day to explore this crazy,
beautiful, gossamer-like world, however much money
is in your bank account, however many certificates
you put up on your wall!

It is the overwhelming bliss of giving without
expectation, loving without need, opening up to
adventures you never thought possible, feeling the
fear yet taking the leap in spite of the words of
warning from the ones who call themselves "sane." It
is the crazy plunge into the unknown, the rush of life
you feel on the in-breath, the profound rest you feel
on the out-breath, the excitement of knowing that
nothing that is real can be lost, and nothing that is
lost was really yours to begin with. It is feeling deeply
alive, connected, and at Home, no matter what the
circumstances, however hard the challenges, however
impossible the odds.

You can have all the earthly riches imaginable, you can be at the very top of the world's ladder of success; yet if you are not in tune with this universal abundance, not in sync with the preciousness of existence, not in touch with who you really are, not in love with the simple feeling of being alive, you are in the deepest poverty.

It is not worldly wealth that raises us out of poverty, but awakening to our vastness. It is not more money that we need in the end, but more Love, that universal Love that holds all beings in all worlds in its infinite embrace. Yes, money helps. It increases worldly comforts. And yes, there is nothing wrong with working to make more money; behind the desire for more money may just be the desire to increase the prosperity of the whole world, to uplift everyone and everything in abundance. But if we are talking about true happiness, we must look beyond the visible, and into the eyes of the Beloved.

Let this be the year you giggle more, laugh more, weep more, fall to your knees more in gratitude and in silliness, and see the preciousness in the passing of things. When you become like a little child, you will enter the Kingdom of Heaven, and the Kingdom is already here, friend, disguised as an ordinary year, an ordinary day, an ordinary moment, waiting for your eyes to open wide to its abundant gifts.

93　Beautiful Devastation

How are you supposed to carry on with your life
when such beauty exists?

A bird chirping its morning song of joy and
heartache, the last kiss from a loved one before they
depart for destinations unknown, a broken promise
or a broken heart transmuting unexpectedly into
grace, an unexpected kindness, a single note in
a familiar tune that takes your breath away, an
emotion of great fragility greeting you as you wake.
How are you supposed to be able to hold all this in
your tiny heart?

One step at a time. One step at a time. Make
room for occasional devastation. Sometimes it's okay
to be unable to stand. Let life call you closer, and
closer still.

94　How to Fall in Love

When you shift your focus
from what is absent
to what is present,
from what is missing
to what has been given,
from what you are not
to who you are,
from the ravages of linear time
to the immediacy of Now,
you are reconnecting
with love, truth, and beauty,
and abundance is yours,
effortlessly.

For in truth,
nothing is lacking where you are,
nothing is missing from the present scene
    of the movie of your life,
and you are forever full,
and at the point of completion.

The only reason
you cannot find Oneness
is because you never left.

The day is just waiting to be lived.

So breathe in life, friend,
breathe in life.

95 Abundance Is Yours

What you truly seek has always been seeking you. And what you never really wanted, you'll never receive anyway, or it will leave soon enough.

Move in the world not from a place of lack, always focused on the goal, measuring how far or near you are, but from a place of presence, slowness, trust. Relax, breathe, and open your arms wide to life today. Be soft and receptive, and stay close to doubt. Everything will come to you.

You'll get to taste it all, the success and the failure, the pleasure and the pain, the highest joy and the most profound heartache. Make a nest for all these lost fragments of your ancient and infinite self. Trust what comes and trust what goes. Trust what stays and trust what leaves. Trust even the doubt.

What you truly seek is seeking you as much as you are seeking it, for you are only looking in to a mirror. You seek your own presence, and you were never divided from it. As you find it, you are found. As you know it, you are known. You are embraced as deeply as you embrace.

Abundance is yours, effortlessly, then. The miracle of each breath, every beat of the heart, every sensation pulsating, fluttering, tingling in the body. A joy, a sorrow, an explosion of creativity. An unexpected connection, a sudden loss. A new chance to meet yourself. A new day to taste all that life has to offer, to give all you have to give.

A fresh new moment now, offered for free. A priceless gift, given. Full, complete like an ocean, you play with desire as she rises and falls, like a beloved wave in your vastness.

PART IX **Rest in Love**

96 Love Is Here

Love has nothing to do with the other person.
    It is closer to you.
Love is electricity, raw, wild, uncontainable.
    It is what you are.
Love does not split itself between the lover
    and their beloved, for that would make two.
Love does not long for "the perfect lover,"
    for the perfect lover is already here.
Love is prior to the imagination of separation,
    prior to the urge to possess or contain.
Love comes before grasping, grabbing, striving,
    needing, desiring, clinging.
Love does not try to make itself lovable.
Love does not strive to be worthy.

In truth, I cannot love you.
You cannot give me love nor can you take it away.
I cannot seek love, nor can I hold it.
Nor will I ever lose it,
this universal love that makes the stars shine,
that turns the soil, that holds us all in its
    infinite embrace,
that knows no death.

In the place where we once imagined separation,
    in the dark place,
we find only absolute intimacy with life,
unspeakable closeness with every breath,
    sensation, feeling,
with anyone—friend, lover, stranger, brother,
    sister—who enters the field.
Every doubt, every moment of sadness,
    every surge of fear, has a home here.

There is no loneliness when you are the Earth
    and all its inhabitants.

I cannot love you, friend, for I am what you are,
    and we are too close to be divided now.
Prior to time, way before space, we meet, in the
    absence of world.
Two cannot become one, if there were never two.
Come into my heart, there is endless room.
There is nothing to seek, and nothing to lose,
    here in the vastness.

97   I Am Love

You never fall in love with another person; the other person is only a catalyst and a messenger. You fall in love with Life itself and her staggering possibilities. You sink more deeply into your own sweet Presence, the unchanging vastness at the core of your being. And you credit another person. Or you blame them when you disconnect. But it's all you, and all for you, and for your healing, and theirs, too, and the salvation of this world.

It's a rediscovery of who you truly are, beyond the mask, behind the carefully constructed facades, the infinitely creative defenses designed for only one reason: to win you love, or prevent you from losing it, as if love were ever something you could win or lose.

And so you simply fall into love, into your nature, your heart, which is their heart, for there is no separation in the vastness, no double vastness but only One. There is no need to leave yourself to know what you are looking for. You are the One, never a seeker of love but its source and destination and reason, and you can move and have your being in the world as that.

And you can shine like the sun, and sometimes others will shine with you, or they will not shine; they will seek your shining or fear it; yet you will keep shining anyway, for you are in love with the shining itself.

To know love is to know that love can never be found, for it shines in the looking, the finding, the losing, in the strength of the shining, even in the stillness of the night.

As Freud realized, you cannot love what you desire, and you cannot desire what you love. For love is always closer, more intimate, at less of a distance than desire, unable to objectify or itself be objectified.

The sun has given her light freely for billions of years, delighting in the life she brings to all beings; a joyful warrior of love, she is in relationship, first and foremost, with her own shining.

98   The Heart

The heart is an unlimited room.
There is always enough room
for the contents of this moment.

The highest joy,
the deepest agony,
thoughts that won't stop spinning,
the heart can hold it all.

Embrace is all it knows.
Space is its nature.
It needs no time.
It asks nothing.
It gives everything in return.

It is home
for all those lost parts of yourself,
for all the abandoned pieces
of the puzzle of "you."

Remembering the heart,
acknowledging its presence,
honoring its invincibility,
savoring its warmth.

Like a deep exhale,
like a cold drink on a scorching day,
like a fond memory of a loved one
long since departed.

They gave you a name
before you were named,
and that name was Love.

And you will never understand
until you stop trying.

99   Giant

You are resting, little one.
Rest easy.
My heart is encased in yours.

You are breathing, little one.
Breathe without shame or fear.
I am here until you breathe your last.

I would take a thousand arrows,
I would sacrifice a thousand pleasures
to protect your freedom,
to give you life.

We may never meet.
You may never know my name.
But I will show you
how giant a love can be.

100 Karma Chameleon

If somebody treats you with unkindness, if they judge or criticize you, it's likely they have endured similar treatment from others in the past, and they are only repeating unconscious patterns in search of a love they cannot find. They will continue to repeat until they wake up from their nightmare of projection, and truly see who you are, who they are, who we all are.

An excuse? No. A way to begin to find compassion for them, to stop taking their behavior so personally and so seriously, to begin to break the cycle of violence? Perhaps. And that "perhaps" is everything when it comes to loving each other.

101 The Harder You Burn, The Brighter You Shine

A life without any kind of pain is no life at all. As the ancient myths and legends remind us, there cannot be true growth without the heroic journey into darkness. Pain has the power to destroy ego and its dreams and bring great humility, to awaken compassion and guide us directly into the warmth of our own sweet presence. An enlightenment that promises total detachment from our humanity, a permanent state of pure uninterrupted bliss free from any kind of pain, is an enlightenment rooted in profound fear, a nightmare of ego.

For billions of years, the sun has given us its awesome power for free. Think of all the burning it has had to endure in order to shine so brightly and give us life.

We are tempted to turn away from our raw, burning hearts, our broken bodies, and confused minds, and fixate on a secondhand future goal. But in the end, our burning is exactly what will make our light shine even more brightly. If we can just stay close . . .

Only love matters, friend. All our spiritual knowledge and attainments, all the drama of the "I know more than you" mind, all the spiritual posturing of the frightened ego, just pale in comparison to the simple joy of true connection, and the peace that comes from knowing that you are nothing less than a burning sun.

102   Two by Two

A great flood is coming.
Construct a safe haven for your loved ones.
Build an ark deep in your heart.

Let all the creatures in, two by two.
Doubt and certainty, joy and sorrow.
Confusion and clarity, bliss and boredom.
Everything sacred, everything profane.
Every thought, every sensation, every feeling.
Every neglected fragment of your ancient self.
Craft an ark of love, vast enough to hold it all.

Let each pair of opposites find sanctuary in your non-
    dual vastness.

Sail toward a gentler world.

103   Newborn

In a hospital ward, on an ordinary November morning, my sweet octogenarian father holds his newborn baby granddaughter for the first time. Just a moment, but enough time for universes to be born.

"Who are you?" they ask each other without words, and no answer comes, and no answer is needed, perhaps. He just holds her, as he was held so long ago, and he laughs, and he speaks words filled with softness and hope and prayers for a good life, and he forgets the transience of things and the struggle of his own tender heart. As Dad's memory fades away, as he slowly rests in his true Home, here at the edge of worlds, they meet. Although they appear to be so different, they feel each other's living presence, and know each other as the same thing in different bodies.

Love is all that matters, friend, all that ever mattered, and we are fools to imagine otherwise.

Fathers, granddaughters, the birth and death of stars, parents relieved to meet their special ones, broken hearts, fading memories, separation and union, the world spinning merrily on its axis, and as I always say, love can only recycle itself.

I surrender. I surrender to it all. Even in the midst of broken hearts and new beginnings, love knows no limits, no bounds, no endings. There is so much beauty here on this strange planet, and who would have thought we'd be lucky enough to witness it?

104　The Fall

Every dream you ever had of "love" will burn in the fall.
The security—the security and the hopes you had
for the future will burn, and the flames will laugh
in their faces as you fall. And the promises—you'll
question every one of those, leaving no concept
untouched, unquestioned, in your descent.
Falling . . . past futures imagined and forgotten,
and all the many versions of the past you have spun, and
all the things you were spoon-fed, all those beautiful
teachings of love written by gods and gurus
. . . none of those will help you now . . .
Through layers of effluent and vomit, blood and spit,
through all the detritus of the seeker, sacred and
profane, the rotting mass of unanswered prayers
and regrets, and through all the unspoken words,
the things you stored in your heart but never said to the
ones you loved, the secrets you kept hidden out of
fear, the longings from which you ran, the heartbreak
you refused to feel, the love from which you guarded
yourself in pursuit of some illusory security . . .
Hitting the bottom, waking up spluttering,
surprised to be alive still, overjoyed to be alive still, it
will all become clear, that love was the only reason,
the only answer, the only meaning, and you will kiss the
ground, you will celebrate the ground, you will never
forget the ground again.
You will remember, she held you as you fell, she
held you in her arms as you fell.

105   Be My Valentine, World

Love is not a feeling. If love were a feeling,
it would come and go, like in a great drama.
Love is not a thought. If love were a thought,
it would have an opposite. Love is too vast to be
    contained in thought.
Love is not a belief. If love were a belief, you would
    doubt it.
And who would believe that?
Love is not a state. If love were a state,
you could enter or leave it. Or fall out of it.
Love is not an experience. If love were an experience,
it would begin and end, and you would long
    for its return.
Love is not something you find. If love were
    something you found, you could lose it, too,
    so you'd have to cling to it for dear life.
Love is simpler, kinder, closer, less dramatic.
    Less urgent, more present.
Love is the space in which everything appears.
    Every thought, every sensation, every feeling,
    pleasurable and painful, blissful, boring,
    erotic, gentle and intense, all are held in
    love's vast embrace.

Yes, *you* are the space for it all, intimate with every
    breath, in love with every beat of the heart, every
    sound, every smell, every sensation in the body,
    every fiery urge, every moment of life.

Feeling like you're in love or not feeling like you're in
love, either way, you are in love with the bliss and
the boredom of existence, with the certainty and the
doubt of it, with the pleasure and the pain, with
the success and the failure, with the seeking and the
resting, with every sacred movement of this
astonishing dream world.

All that can be had, can be lost. All that you can gain,
can be taken away. All that you can build up, can
turn to dust overnight. All that can be created,
can also be destroyed.
Only love remains. Only love.
Not a feeling, not a thought, not a belief, not a state, not
an experience, not something that you "have,"
not something that you're "in" or "out" of, not
something that you "get" from others (despite
the romantic myths we are sold), but the endless
embrace of all of this.
Love is you. You, before you were named, before you
were even born, before the universe came into form.
You. You are the One. The One you have always sought.
The unsilenceable call of the heart. The cry from
deep within. The fragile stillness in the middle
of the night.
You will never abandon yourself again.

Love is not supposed to always feel "safe." A
supernova does not always feel "safe."

Love is not the product they force-feed you via
TV or in the movies. Love is not a Hallmark card,
all smiling faces and warm feelings and promises we
can't be certain to keep.

Love is a furnace, destruction, unsparing. It
will burn anything in its path. It is unsentimental,
reducing to ashes the unreal, the pretense, the lies,
the half truths, anything that is not immediate,
alive, firsthand, touchable. Love will smash every
preconceived version of love, the fairy tales we so
badly wanted to believe in. Love has no interest
in our hopes, fantasies, plans. Everything is fuel.
Everything is there for the taking.

The vastness of love cannot be reduced to an
excited nervous system, butterflies in the stomach,
stolen kisses, and the joy of togetherness. Love
also takes into its ancient heart that raging sense
of loneliness, that heart torn open and unable to
be mended, the abandoned one, the lost one, the
unwanted. Love can hold a raw panic in its gut, a
wave of terror in the middle of the night when
the kids are sleeping, a most profound boredom
appearing out of nowhere. Love is uncertainty, too.
Love is feeling as unsafe as you felt when you were
first thrust into this uncontrollable world, torn out of

the security of the womb, battle-weary, but breathing on your own for once, victorious.

Forget your fantasies of love, friend. Love will come for you there on the cross. Under the Bodhi tree. On the dirty streets of Calcutta. In the prison they say you'll never leave. On the operating table. The killing fields. Love cannot be destroyed, yet destroys the love-dreams of mind. Love cannot be lost, cannot be taken, yet allows the loss, too, outlives all that is not you. Love is not a feeling because feelings come and go, and love does not, or else it is not love, but a fleeting dream.

Yet this is not true. For love would also take the shape of all that is not love; her ingenious invitation. Even the conditional is a movement of the Unconditioned, for nothing is rejected here, including rejection.

Do you know how vast your heart is? How your heart was formed with all these other hearts in a place of unbearable pressure at the core of a dying star? How your heart is made from the same stuff as my heart, the heart of every living being? The dinosaur, the mollusk, the whale, the creatures of darkness that crawl in the ocean's depths. The saint and the sinner. How it is all actually the same heart, beating, the heartbeat of a universe, expansion, contraction, gain, loss, birth, death, rebirth, a cycle as ancient as life itself, reinventing itself in every moment. Do you know a love so huge it would spill out of itself as an entire cosmos, burning, burning, raging for itself, devouring itself, chasing itself, seeking itself, beckoning, crawling, destroying all that it is not, yet creating that, too, and delighting in the creation? An utterly destructive, infinitely creative love that you can feel pounding in you in every moment? A love that will never let you settle for anything less?

Grandmother disappeared into it. They all did. The billions that came before. The ones who left. The ones you tried to forget. They all returned to your heart, nourished you.

Your heart is overflowing; your path is clear; you are unstoppable now.

107 Love Song to Myself

You are the one I wake with every morning. The one I breathe with, the one whose every heartbeat I feel as my own. You are the one I walk with, the one I speak and sing with, the one who stays with me through every waking moment of every sacred day. You are the one I get sick with, the one I cry with, the one whose anger and joy and doubt surges through me like fire. You are the one I will die with, the one whose arms I return to. You are the one I see in every face, shining through every pair of eyes, shimmering through the silences, the trails of dust and the spaces in the canopy. You are my constant companion, my home, my reason, my joy, my life. We cannot be divided, we cannot be two, and even One is too many for us.

I sing this song to myself, disappearing into the song, and I am never alone.

An Ocean of Love

In love, there is loss. Yet there is also fullness, beyond the ravages of temporality.

Love is the loss of time. Past and future fall away, and all that remains is simplicity, no division between lover and beloved, seer and seen. An object ceases to be an object; a person ceases to be a person, for no boundary can exist in this intimacy, no division at all, no duality.

A world is lost, a world falls away, a fire burns in which time's dramas are incinerated. And this love is not personal, it is not contained, it cannot be passed from one entity to another. It can only be remembered, not generated. Revealed, never received.

The ground opens up, and we fall.

In the eyes of a stranger, or while contemplating the mysteries of a flower, or on beholding a piece of art in a gallery, and often suddenly, unexpectedly, without warning, love swallows you whole.

You recognize yourself. What is *out there* is really *in here*. Boundaries melt. Great walls crumble.

Somewhere, out across the ocean, in the vastness of night, something unseen and unknown calls to you from the depths.

Never leave yourself, friend. There is nowhere to go.

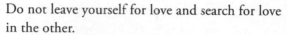

Do not leave yourself for love and search for love
in the other.

Love is not an object; it cannot be given nor
taken away.

Love is not a feeling, a state, or a peak experience,
but what you are, Presence itself.

Do not confuse love with attraction. Attraction
comes and goes, can fade over time, can diminish or
surge like a volcano, unexpectedly.

Do not confuse love with longing. Longing is also
impermanent, transitory.

Do not confuse love with feelings of bliss,
pleasure, an excited nervous system. These passing
states cannot last; it is not in their nature. Even
promises, given with such certainty today, with the
best of intentions, can fade tomorrow, or be broken,
or forgotten.

Love, however, does not fade. Love cannot
diminish over time. Love is not a commodity, a
shifting form. Love is a field, a field within and
without and in between us; a field in which thoughts,
feelings, even the most seemingly solid plans for the
future, can appear and disappear. Love holds hope
as much as loss, excitement as much as boredom,
crushing disappointment as much as bliss.

Love is the field for the shifting forms, the ground that holds us as we walk, sit, talk or do not, feel what we feel in each other's presence, go about the business of our day, plan, eat, hope, say good-bye, try to love.

Love is greater than us. We do not generate it with words and deeds, or even intentions, but we are continually embraced by it, held in its vastness, no matter what we do, or do not.

We are married, we divorce; we are friends, we are lovers; we break up, we break together; we are born, we die; the field endures.

Nobody has ever given us love; that is the great illusion. We have simply remembered the field in each other's presence, sometimes, recognized eternity in the midst of the everyday, then credited each other. Love never came from outside of us; we simply touched our own presence, fell into the love that we are, and cannot not be. And nobody ever took love away from us; we simply forgot the field, and "blamed" the other, and looked for love again, feeling its absence, lost in a narrative of "lost love," caught up in the drama of the lonely one.

Yet love was still there, even in its own apparent absence; it was present, even in the loss. It cannot be broken; a wave cannot crush the ocean.

Do not seek love, do not look for the light, but be it, offer it; the joy of loving another is infinitely greater than the joy of fearfully seeking or clinging to another's love, for deep down you know it is only an illusion that what you have always longed for could ever have come from outside of your own heart. You are the One; you have always been the One.

The search ends exactly where it began—in presence. From love's perspective, nothing happened at all.

110   Ghosts of the Heart

No one can ever be erased from your heart, for once you have been touched by someone and touched them in return, once you have held them so tenderly in your arms and been held in return, and known them as yourself, and let them into you, let them *see* you, there is an indelible memory in the heart, however hard you try to forget them, however hard you now push them away. For the heart knows no time, no absence, no separation, no mistakes, and we are forever inseparable from all we have experienced or run away from. We are haunted by the past until we face it, pursued by all we have shut out.

The closed heart, which seems at first like great self-protection, soon feels like great self-imprisonment. There is a pain greater than pain; the pain of running away from our pain, dividing ourselves from ourselves and pursuing some secondhand ideal of "love." There cannot be two. There is only One. Love cannot be divided, yet we run until our legs ache.

And at last, we fall to our knees, exhausted. And then, perhaps, our hearts open. And we cannot change the past, we cannot erase what transpired, but we can fall in love with the present, with where we are, the kind of falling we were always seeking in time.

"Fall into me," it whispers. "It is safe to fall. Let go."

And the sad ghosts running toward you only ever wanted to be allowed into the brilliance of your presence. Their journey at an end, they die a beautiful death in your arms, fading to light.

You are forgiven, in Presence, and there was nothing to forgive.

111   Love's Brilliant Return

And the night belongs to us, and the dawn, too, and
we shall never again forget this grace we have been
given, never again abandon this day in pursuit of
another. Love is not something you find; it is like an
energy, flowing, sometimes soft, barely perceptible,
pulsating, sometimes surging, volcanic, spilling out
everywhere, filling the cracks in the sidewalk, the
walls we erected to keep us apart, bubbling like a
brook, finding its way into every space, unstoppable,
unstoppable, searching for its source, looking for its
home, flowing through trees, lakes, people, flowing
into the open skies, past galaxies, backward and
forward through time.

A baby is born; a man takes his last breath in a
hospital somewhere, who knows where; an army rises,
is defeated, rises; a slave breaks his chains; great beasts
walk the Earth, not knowing how close they have
come to the fires. Stars are born and explode, your first
birthday, your graduation, the death of your mother,
your father, weeping into handkerchiefs, challenges you
felt you would never overcome, and you overcame,
and somewhere in the middle of the night, out across
some vast ocean, somewhere in the dark recesses of
your heart, or perhaps near the limits of the known
universe, I don't know, she remembers, she turns
back, remembering the source, yes, she remembers
the source now, and she turns back, not seeking

but falling, not pushing but allowing herself to be
pulled, and she falls back, through the light and the
darkness, through the sewage of a million lost worlds,
through mystery, through layers of bliss and pain, into
you, into your ancient heart, into her home. She has
traveled to the ends of worlds, beyond time and space,
through indescribable horrors and ecstasies, and she
has found you again, where she left you, where the
search began.

You take a breath now, you feel the heart beating,
you feel your belly rise and fall, and this is not just
some ordinary movement, some moment in a series
of moments, this is eternity moving, breathing,
infinite in nature, finite in form yet infinite in heart,
and it was always you, it was always you, sought and
found, lost and discovered.

It is just an ordinary day in your life, kids to feed,
bills to pay, feelings to feel, but now you know, now
you cannot forget, despite the dream, despite the
journey, the dawn belongs to you, and the night, too,
and every call of every creature, and every pair of eyes,
all yourself looking, wondering, thinking of home,
and you shall never again forget this grace you
have been given, never again abandon this day in
pursuit of another, never seek love outside your own
pumping heart, never doubt what you intuitively
knew when mother ejected you into this world,

kicking and screaming, broken and bloody but brilliantly yourself, that you are not a mistake, you are not a damn mistake, you are nature, you are whole, and worthy, worthy of the kind of love that travels eons and light-years and pulls itself through the shadows and the shit to return. From you, she birthed herself; to you, she comes running.

Home, Mother, Home!

112   Naked Love

You say you love me. You say you care. You say a lot
of things, but words are cheap, and I am worthy of
the kind of love that builds galaxies.

If you would see my open wounds, my scars.
If you would see my dark places, know my secrets. If
you would see my fantasies, my strange thoughts,
the impulses I have not been able to erase. The
uncomfortable feelings I try to hide. The desperate
longings, the empty feelings that haven't left.

The rage that burns. The grief that aches.

If you would know the things I keep buried in
my heart, the things I cannot speak. If you would
see the wrinkles, the folds, the pigmentation, the
lumps and lesions, spots and sores. The growths,
the imperfections, the errant hairs. The fluids whose
flow I cannot stem, the secretions, the smells, the
terrors of the night.

If you would see me naked, shaking, stripped
of my image, my make-up, my foundations and
sprays and cover-ups, my pretenses, my defenses,
my barriers and walls; with no hiding, no games,
no masks, no persona, no part to play and nothing
to lose.

If you would see it all, raw, uncensored,
uncontrolled.

Would you still love me? Would your heart open?
Would you see ugliness, or would you see art?

A vulnerable heart. Longing to be met. Perfect in my imperfection.

You say you love me. You say you care. You say a lot of things, but words are cheap, and I am worthy of the kind of love that builds galaxies.

113

What They Taught You

They taught you that you were small.
They told you that you were incomplete, limited.
That there was something missing. Some deficiency.
Something "wrong" with you.
(They believed in "right" and "wrong.")
That you were "less than." And others were "more than."

They sold you a lie.
They fed you a nightmare.
That love was conditional. That you had to work for it.
Earn it. Be "good enough" for it.
That the source of your self-worth was outside of you.
And was outside of your control.
And was dependent upon doing better. Being
    faster. Smarter. Louder. Quieter. Being taller,
    prettier, more accomplished. Achieving better
    grades. Climbing high. Descending when
    told. Making more. Having more. Money.
    Certificates. Titles. Praise. Applause. Building
    a better image. Constructing a better you. A
    better version. An upgrade.
It was all a lie.
You were lovable exactly as you were. In your
    original form.
From the beginning, you were whole. And complete.
And worthy. Worthy of love.
Worthy of good quality attention.

Worthy of empathy.
Worthy of safety.
Worthy of dignity, respect.
Your feelings mattered, even the uncomfortable
ones. Your body was beautiful, even with its
imperfections. Your voice was sacred, even when
they didn't agree.
Your success mattered, and your failures were also pure.
Your in-breath mattered. Your out-breath, too.

They taught you that you were small.
They told you that you were incomplete, limited.
That there was something missing. Some deficiency.
Something "wrong" with you.
That you were "less than." And others were "more than."

They were mistaken, always.

Yet forgive them, Father; they knew not what they
were doing.
For they were taught the same.

114

How to Open Your Heart

Do not *try* to open your heart.

That would be a subtle movement of aggression toward your immediate embodied experience. Never tell a closed heart it must be more open; it will shut more tightly to protect itself, feeling your resistance and disapproval. A heart unfurls only when conditions are right; your demand for openness invites closure. This is the supreme intelligence of the heart.

Instead, bow to the heart in its current state. If it's closed, let it be closed; sanctify the closure. Make it safe; safe even to feel unsafe.

Trust that when the heart is ready, and not a moment before, it will open, like a flower in the warmth of the sun. There is no rush for the heart.

Trust the opening and the closing, too, the expansion and the contraction; this is the heart's way of breathing: *safe, unsafe, safe, unsafe;* the beautiful fragility of being human, and all held in the most perfect love.

115   Life: The Price of Admission

You will emerge, bloody, broken, bruised, but alive.
They will tell you you're on a planet called Earth.
They will give you a name. Somebody else's name.
They will teach you what they think is true.
You will learn to speak a particular language, not of
    your choosing. You will be taught your family's
    beliefs, values, codes of conduct. (Don't take these
    as absolute truth; it's just their version of truth.)
They will praise you or blame you. Support you or not.
    They will give you gifts or take gifts away. They will
    call you wrong, bad, selfish, evil. They will call you
    the best, wonderful, a genius, their savior.
Don't buy into their names, their judgments, good
    or bad. You are alive. You cannot be contained or
    controlled. Or defined by words.
You will love and lose love. Your heart will break,
    often. You will touch the greatest ecstasy, the
    depths of melancholy. Those you love will die.
You will question your reality, your identity, even
    your sanity.

You will sometimes feel that you cannot go on. You will go on.

You will wonder about your purpose. Find a purpose, lose it. Inhabit a role, shed it. Trust someone, and the trust will be broken. Or will remain unbroken. Or you will fall to your knees. And stand. And fall. And stand again. And keep going.

You will taste all of life, the dark and the light. All of life will surge through you, the joy and the sorrow, the boredom and the bliss, the certainty and the doubt, great excitements and the terrors of the deep.

You will touch others and be touched in return.

You will dance and sing and crumble in despair.

You will weep and laugh and fall into the Mystery.

And in the end, you will cry out:

"I have lived! I have lived!"

116　Mother

They said you were growing "inside" me. But I knew better. You were closer than that. My body *was* yours. Your breath *was* my breath. Your heart *was* mine.

"You must be happy," they said. "Congratulations. You'll be a wonderful mother."

I didn't know. Great terrors welled up inside me. Ecstasies, too.

At times, I felt such a profound loneliness. Like nobody understood, even my closest friends, my family, my husband.

My pain was your pain, little one. My joys, my sorrows, my fears, my hungers, all yours. And yours, all mine.

Strange sensations. Aches. Tenderness, twitches. Mood swings. Nausea. Jesus, the constant nausea. Blood, everywhere. Backaches. Heartburn. Everything on fire.

If I'm honest, there were times I blamed you. Wanted you gone from me, the ultimate betrayal. You broke my heart and shattered my dreams. An old life gone, a new life growing. A death, a birth, a crisis of faith. Sometimes I didn't know if I still wanted you. I can admit it now.

Yet there were times I needed you so badly. Times I couldn't imagine living without you. Times you were all I had in this world. You were my reason for taking another breath, my reason for staying.

Cracking open. The fear of myself. Fear of the things I could never share. Dark things. Visions. Movements in the night. The snake, the bat, the velociraptor. Demons, devils, enticing me away. Unknown things coming for my soul. The unconscious becoming conscious. Messages. The dead coming alive. Movements of the planets in deep space. Strange connections, coincidences, inexplicable happenings. Rumblings in the void. The collective fears of every mother. Trying to hold it all together. For you. For you.

What to eat, what not to eat. To sleep, to wake. To move, to rest. To keep you safe. To keep you so safe. To keep myself safe. How to move as you grew.

Everyone giving their advice. Leave me alone. Shut up. Leave me alone, all of you.

My hand on you. Skin pulling itself tighter. Skin stretching, folding, peeling. Layers coming off.

Was that you moving? Do I feel you? Strange visions, feelings I can't explain. New feelings. Confusing. Unbearable sometimes.

Keep it in. Hold it all together. Put on a brave face.

"You must be so happy. Congratulations. You'll be a wonderful mother."

And then the day you came out. Pushing, pushing, and you, not coming, not coming. Pushing, and a fuck-the-world kind of pain, and no, I don't think men could understand, really I don't.

Rupture. Flesh breaking. Gushing, spewing, the searing of a universe.

Bloody, bruised, naked but alive, there you were! Mind stopped. Mind gone.

Mine. Not mine any longer. Yet mine, so mine. And beautiful. Beautiful. Perfect. Shattered, yes, but perfect.

My heart breaks a thousand times, and you mend it a thousand times over.

You had a face, your own. Such a face. Legs, arms, too. Eyes that knew. Eyes like mine. You grew from inside me but appeared outside. You shape shifter, you miracle, you little boy.

You breathed for yourself. My little boy, breathing for himself. And suddenly, I missed the days we breathed together. Nostalgia for those days. But I loved that you breathed on your own. The joy and the sorrow of it, I cannot explain. I could barely hold it all in my exhausted heart.

Dependent, independent. One, but not the same.

My son, my sweet little boy, I don't know if you were born that day, if you let go of me, or if an old life died, or all three. Why was my heart breaking, when everyone around was weeping for joy? Did you know the answer? My little boy. My slimy, bloody, screaming-for-your-life, announcing-your-arrival-to-all-who-would-listen little boy. Cutting us apart, yet we could never be apart. We are two hearts made of the same heart, two breaths that once were indistinguishable. I would die for you, give you my heart, my brain, my face, my everything.

I am your mother, and you are my son.

And if King Solomon pronounced his judgment, I would not even need to think. The answer is yes, my love, the answer is yes. Have him, have him, have him you liar, have all of him, not half of him but all of him, and keep him safe, and love him the way I love him, and I will hold him in my heart, and he will find me, I know he will find me, one day, one day, he will break his chains and he will find me, he will find his way home, for his body was mine, his breath was my breath, and our hearts still beat as one.

117   In Love, Whether You Win or Lose, You Win

Child, know that I will love you if you succeed. And know that I will love you equally if you fail.

For failure is only a thought, and your worthiness is not tied to external things. You are not less because you make less, or know less, or win less, or own less. And you are not more because you have more, or attain more, or succeed more. The in-breath is no better than the out-breath, my love, the falling is beautiful and the rising, too. The snow and the rain are as glorious as the summer sunshine; the smallest pool of water is as great as the Pacific Ocean, and the Earth's core has survived the most outrageous triumphs and disasters. If you try and win, experience it fully, taste it fully, and learn to love the taste. But if failure and disappointment come to visit, if heartbreak and loss arise in your precious heart, if despair and a deep loneliness surge out of nowhere, if they mock and ridicule you, if they neglect and abandon you, if they don't see you as you long for them to see you, know I will not abandon you; know you are as worthy as you ever were, and as lovable, and as extraordinarily beautiful, and as whole. Learn to love the taste of the dark as well as the light. Taste all of life my love; you were built to hold it all, and your heart is vast, and your courage breathtaking.

I teach this love to you, and you will teach it to your children, and on and on until the end of the world.

In love, you are victorious!

118   Our Last Chance to Love

And because the earth could crack open at any
moment pulling us downward into her fire, and
because there are so many things in our hearts we
will never be able to put into words, and because
the dinosaurs lived and loved and died too fast, and
because we are all here so fleetingly, perched on this
fragile blue planet spinning in infinite dust, and
because of all these things, let today be the day we
finally speak our truth, even if we must tremble and
sweat and wonder what the hell we're doing; the day
we finally listen, even if we don't like what we hear;
the day we finally receive the gift of life, oxygen in
our lungs, our feet on the ground, our hearts open to
each other, to pain and to pleasure and to possibility,
the earth ready to crack open at any moment,
sucking us into her ancient burning core.

PART
X

**Rest
in Silence**

119 Breathe

Slow down, friend.
Breathe.
In, out.
In, out.

Sink into the vastness of Presence.
Life is only a moment.
Answers do not arrive on demand.
We are on an ancient schedule here.

The teaching is simple:

Slow down, friend.
Breathe.
In, out.
In, out.

A Mindful Moment of Calm

Stop. Just for a moment.

Feel the magic of the in-breath, the out-breath, one breath at a time. Feel the belly rising and falling in its own sweet time, like an ocean wave. Feel the air moving through the nostrils, down the back of the throat. Feel how deeply the air moves into the body.

Notice what's alive in your body right now. Come out of the story of past and future, of regret and anticipation, of "what's not here" and "what should be here," and give some kind attention to the dance of physical sensation happening here, where you are. A fluttery feeling in the stomach, now. A tension in the shoulders, or a pressure in the forehead, now. A light, excited feeling in the chest, now.

If you find an area of discomfort, that's okay—be present with it. Don't try to get rid of it, make it go away. Don't label it, or judge it as "bad" or "negative." Right now, don't even try to "heal" it. (Sometimes even "healing" can be a subtle form of resistance.) And if you notice any resistance, any non-acceptance, allow that to be here, too. Remain curious, fascinated. Be curious even about your lack of curiosity, fascinated with your boredom. Even boredom has its place in life.

Allow all thoughts to come and go. Thoughts are clouds, you are the sky, the space for all thoughts, not their enemy. Don't try to delete thoughts or even quiet them down. Embrace their glorious noise, and know they are not who you truly are.

Don't try to make anything happen. You're not seeking a different experience or state. Become curious about this experience, this state! This day. This hour. This moment. This immediacy. Where you are. What's it like to be alive, here and now? What's it like to be you, uniquely you? Meet this moment in its freshness.

You cannot be truly curious about your immediate, embodied, present experience and be stuck in a story of fear and regret at the same time. If premature conclusions are the dis-ease, if fear and stress are the symptoms, open-hearted curiosity is the only true medicine. This moment is your anchor, your cosmic home in a chaotic ever-changing world, your calm in the midst of the storm, and storms have always passed.

121   Birds of the Mind

Thoughts are not the truth. And ultimately, thoughts are not even yours; they are not personal, not who you truly are. They are only voices, sounds, suggestions, judgments, opinions of the mind, coming and going all the time, like a flock of birds singing, every bird singing a different tune; a different opinion, suggestion, perspective.

You are not the birds; you are the wide-open space in which the birds can sing, the awareness that holds the birds, the silence underneath and in-between, the silence infusing the birdsong.

Do not try to silence the birds (for that makes them sing even more loudly in protest) or destroy them (for they are only parts of yourself longing for some gentleness), but allow them to sing, and fly away, and return; therein lies your power, and your freedom, and therefore your peace.

The "I am a failure" bird can sing, and the "I am a waste of space" bird can sing, and the "I am the most wonderful bird" bird can sing, and all their in-between friends can sing; and you are a giant nest of awareness, a bird sanctuary, never defined by the chorus of opinions, nor at war with it. You are the great *I Am*, undefinable; the cosmic orchestra pit in love with sound.

122   Tumbling Back into Silence

We try to capture our embodied lives, our ever-changing moment by moment experiences, our moods, our feelings, in *words*. We try to convey the infinite depths of our firsthand experience, using finite concepts, thoughts, little black squiggles on white paper, secondhand, learned sounds that are fixed and unchanging from day to day.

Words are of memory, and memory will never touch the aliveness we know as our own presence and the presence of our immediate world. The raw burning in the gut will never be captured by the word "grief"; the name "anger" will never touch those nameless, fiery explosions within. In many ways, we are unknown men and women to each other, and to ourselves. Therein lies our solitude, and our potential.

Words are powerful tools, yes, yet they remain powerless against the immediacy of living.

There are so many things in your heart you will never be able to express in words. No wonder in Hollywood musicals, they spontaneously burst into song.

Become a poet then, an artist, a wild lover of the silence. Climb into another's heart by reaching into the mysteries of your own.

Dance into the heartbreak and joy, paint an ever-changing picture with your words, and then let them go, tumbling back into silence.

123 The Ashes of Thought

They say you are not your thoughts. So what are you?

Aren't you the unchanging Home for thoughts, the capacity for thoughts, the wide-open space in which thoughts arise and dissolve like waves in the ocean, like clouds on a summer's day? Your ability to hold thoughts as they are born and die does not in itself require thought, and it's what makes you divine. You are not your thoughts, and yet you are inseparable from these intimate and temporary appearances of yourself. Thoughts are your children, too.

Thoughts are not absolute truth, but appearances in That Which Never Appears. They come and go—that is their nature. They are fragments—voices, perspectives, suggestions, ideas, theories, comments, hopes, dreams, memories—but they cannot touch the living vastness of this moment, the immensity of life itself, the wholeness that is sought so fervently. Every thought burns in the fire of Presence. We meet in the ashes of thought, always.

And even that is just a thought.

124 You Are Acceptance Itself

Imagine the perfect movie screen.

It never disappears. It is always present, always "on." It allows all kinds of movies to be projected onto it—war movies, horror movies, comedies, thrillers. Sad movies, joyful movies—the screen provides a welcome home for all of them. The movies come and go, but the screen remains. The screen is never hurt, damaged, or traumatized, even by the most violent or intense movie. It is pure safety. It is unconditional love.

When you are watching a great movie, absorbed in its incredible story, you never notice the screen. You get swept up in the drama. Locations change, scenery shifts, you go forward and even backward in time. Characters are born and die. Wars are fought, tears are shed, connections are made and unmade. All this is happening on a screen that never changes, never moves, never travels in time, is never born, and never dies. The one thing that is essential—the unchanging screen—is never part of the story. And yet, without the movie screen, there could be no story in the first place.

When you walk out of the movie theater, you may think you have been watching a movie all evening, but really, you have only been watching a screen that never moved. You have been staring at something that never changed, never did anything at all, had no story of its own. And yet, at the same time, you feel that you went on a wonderful journey in time and space.

This is the paradox of our lives. We travel, yet we never move.

This living screen is what you really are. Pure awareness prior to concepts, even the concept of "awareness." A constant presence, a present constancy. The movie, the unending dance of concepts, thoughts, sensations, sounds, images, memories, perceptions, urges, impulses, all appears and disappears in your timeless embrace. The movie is constantly moving, but you always remain unmoved, never part of the movie but always allowing it, deeply rooted in the here and now, radically open to the next scene, whatever it turns out to be.

You cannot accept, for you are already acceptance itself; pure receptivity, moment by moment. An invitation, an invocation: *Come, world, arise in me . . .*

125   Thoughts and Feelings

Thoughts and feelings
do not have power over you
until you give them power
by forgetting your nature.

You are the ocean; they are the ever-changing waves.
You are the unfathomable sky; they are the
    passing clouds.
You are the uncontained container;
they are temporary guests in your infinite embrace.

Thoughts and feelings are not you, friend,
but you are vast enough to hold them,
to allow them to come and go,
arise and fall,
emerge, stay for a while, and subside into deep sleep.

You remain, awake.

126 The Field of Meditation

What is meditation?
Pure fascination with this moment,
exactly as it is.
Not adding anything.
Not taking anything away.
No goal.
No seeking.
No meditator, in fact.

Thoughts appearing and falling away,
like waves in a vast ocean.
Sounds coming and going, unexpectedly.
Sensations dancing, fizzling.
Breathing rising and falling,
in this vast field, this wide-open space,
timeless, deathless, free.

What is meditation?
The question itself dissolves . . .

For in your heart of hearts, you are always meditating.

127   The Awakening of You

Yesterday, you died. Today, you awaken.

Open your eyes. A world appears. A world of color, shape, motion, texture, light and shade. A dance of the formless as form, an astonishing carnival presenting itself in your presence, itself unmoving.

The look on a stranger's face. The impossibly blue blue of the bluest sky. That feeling of exquisite vulnerability, of strength and possibility, of mornings that you cannot put into words.

Close your eyes. Let attention drop into the rich world of the body. Feel the immense life surging in all directions, the tingles and the throbs, the aches, the pains, the pleasures, the joyous waves of energy, nameless and mysterious.

Watch the picture show of the mind. The most astonishing movie ever conceived. Time travel is real here. Teleportation, too. In a single thought, quicker than time, you can leap eons and light years, yet remain exactly where you are.

Yesterday, you died. Today, you awaken.

It is immense, this living.

**The Silence of Sound,
The Sound of Silence**

In meditation, do not try to silence sounds or get rid of them, but do not ignore them either.

Stay right in the center; be the unconditionally receptive awareness in which all sounds, pleasant, unpleasant, and neutral, can come and go. Be open to all sounds, near and far, loud and soft. Allow them all to arrive, stay for as long as they need to stay, and leave when they are ready.

Notice how sounds arise on their own, stay for a while, and dissolve in their own time, at their own pace. Sounds are only obeying their own nature, being themselves, perfectly, walking their own path, as all things are.

If a particular sound is distracting you, or annoying you, or bothering you, wonderful! Just notice that annoyance, or irritation, or frustration, or disappointment, and allow it all to be there; it's more grist for the mill.

Notice, it's not the sound itself that's creating the "annoyance," it's the mind's resistance to the sound, the mind's insistence that the sound *shouldn't* be there. Isn't this resistance noisier than the sound itself? What kind of silence would try to silence a sound? Who is distracting whom?

You see, true silence is not the opposite of noise. That is the mind's version of silence, with its obsession with opposites and contrasts and dualities. True silence allows all sounds to come and go; it is the spacious awareness in which even the mind's endless chattering has a home. This loving, all-inclusive silence is what you are. The natural silence of the Heart.

Don't try to silence thoughts and feelings. Don't disturb their precious peace, don't get in their way, or make it unsafe for them to move. Simply know yourself as the deep meditative stillness in which all thoughts and feelings are allowed to come and go, the unconditional acceptance of present experience. The deepest sorrow, the greatest joy, allow them all to flow in and out of the Heart.

129 An Internally-Generated Happiness

Do not search for happiness; it will never come from outside of you, just as the sun's heat is only generated internally. Look outside of your beautiful self, and you will forever be a seeker, clinging to others or resenting them, a victim of fate or chance or the moods, whims, desires, and longings of friends and strangers. Others cannot be controlled or predicted, and their deepest experience is subject to the laws of impermanence. They love you, they forget you, they punish you, they celebrate you, they want you, they lose interest, they move toward you, they move away. They act out and act in. Sometimes they keep their promises, and sometimes they don't; sometimes they tell the truth, and sometimes they can't or won't; and it doesn't matter now, they are let off the hook, they are not responsible for your happiness, and they never were; please do not depend on them. Your self-worth is generated internally, the warmth of presence is always with you now.

Mummy and Daddy called you good or bad, they praised or blamed you, they pushed you or pulled you, they wanted you to be like them or not be like them, they listened or did not, they were overworked or overstressed or intoxicated, they showered you with praise or took praise away without warning; they ignored, neglected or shamed you, they hit you.

they touched you in ways that felt wrong, and you silenced that inner voice that always *knew* it was wrong (to keep their love and keep yourself safe and keep yourself going), but they weren't the holders of truth, and they were in desperate pain, and they didn't know, they didn't know.

And now you are free, or at least you are in touch with that which was always free, because you are present, and your life is your life, and you are breathing, and you are of infinite worth as an expression of the universe, and you are entitled to feel what you feel without shame, even if you feel ashamed. And you have so much to give, and you don't need to forgive, because forgiveness is built-in to presence, and there's nothing to forgive, yet so much to feel, including your inability to forgive, today.

You were always shining, little one, always the Source and the Sun and the Light, and nobody could touch that, nobody could ever take that away. And they never will.

130 A Minute of Mindfulness

Spend a moment feeling your feet on the ground;
notice the way they gently press into the earth.
Silently remind yourself, "I am here. It is Now."

Feel the fullness and heaviness of your entire body,
the weight of it as it is gently drawn downward into the
earth by gravity. Let the body rest, melt, sink, fall
into gravity's unconditional embrace.

Don't try to control your breathing, just notice
its depth, speed, quality, how the belly rises and falls,
rises and falls as it fills with oxygen, empties, refills.
Feel how deeply rooted the breath is in the present
moment. Notice if the breath slows or deepens a
little with some gentle attention.

Now, begin to notice and allow all bodily
sensations: in the forehead, the back of the head, the
jaw, neck and shoulders, the chest, belly, buttocks. If
there is any tension, tightness, contraction, or ache
anywhere, fully allow these sensations, soften into
and around them, breathe into them, allow them
to move, to expand, to intensify, to dissolve, or to
stay. You're not trying to delete or create sensations.
No need to label or judge them either. Just remain
curious, present.

Allow all thoughts and images of the mind. Don't try to stop or silence thoughts about past, present, or future; give them space and breathing room, now. Receive all the ever-changing sounds of the present moment, too; like thoughts, allow them to come and go, arise and fall effortlessly in awareness, like waves in a vast ocean.

Spend a moment fully inhabiting, savoring, welcoming this present scene in the movie of your life as it slowly emerges moment by moment, not adding anything, not removing anything. Simply receive.

Resting for a moment, you may find yourself yawning, shivering, or just going a little floppy as tension dissipates.

You may feel spontaneously sad or joyful, energized or tired. You may feel more present, grounded, connected . . . or you may not. It's all okay; allow your experience to be just as it is, and don't compare it with anything. You are alive and awake to an original moment.

PART XI   Rest in Being Present for Others

131   Healing Happens When You Get Out of the Way

Let people go through what they have to go
through in the present moment! They are tired,
and they want to rest. They are exhausted from the
fight, from the pretense and the lies, from having
to hold everything in and hold everything together
and hold everything up, and great waves of energy
are now moving throughout their bodies.

Stay present with them. Waves of sorrow,
hopelessness, fear, shame, and guilt are surging
now. Let the energies rise up, let their whole bodies
vibrate and shake and quake if they must, let them
wail, scream, roar, laugh. Offer them nothing but the
greatest gift of all: your fearless presence. Stay with
them through each breath, each motion, in every
moment. Hold their hands, but don't try to fix them,
change them, stop them experiencing what they are
experiencing, or give them premature answers.

If you become uncomfortable, or feel like
you want to rush in and "save" them, or "fix"
them, or prevent them from feeling what they
are feeling, or make everything "okay" for them,
own that—it's your need, your discomfort, your
fear, not theirs. Do not treat them like victims
or invalids. Do not confuse them with who you

think they are. Honor the power that moves in them; validate their experience totally. Trust the unpredictable intelligence of healing, and know that their "symptoms" may get worse before they get better; energy may become more intense before it dies down. What appears now as chaos and disintegration may in fact be a necessary release and an intelligent reorganization of blocked systems.

Sometimes our hearts need to break wide open so we are able to hold more life, more powerful love. Let your warm presence remind your friends of their own warm presence, so stable, so fearless, so free, so deeply rooted, grounded, here. Know that who they truly are cannot be broken, not by even the most intense energies, and cannot be fixed, and life never makes mistakes even when life seems like a mistake.

Love is all that matters. The rain falls, stars explode in silence somewhere out in the vastness of space, and here on this tiny planet that someone called Earth, sometimes we meet and hold each other.

132   **To the Sensitive Ones**

Do not be ashamed of your sensitivity!
It has brought you many riches.

You see what others cannot see,
feel what others are ashamed to feel.

You are more open, less numb.
You find it harder to turn a blind eye.
You have not closed your heart,
in spite of everything.

You are able to hold
the most intense highs
and the darkest lows
in your loving embrace.
(You know that neither define you.
Everything passes through.
You are a cosmic vessel.)

Celebrate your sensitivity!
It has kept you flexible and open.
You have remained close to wonder.
And awareness burns brightly in you.

Don't compare yourself with others.
Don't expect them to understand.
But teach them:
It's okay to feel, deeply.
It's okay to not know.
It's okay to play
on the raw edge of life.

Life may seem "harder" for you at times,
and often you are close to overwhelm.
But it's harder still
to repress your overwhelming gifts.

Sensitive ones,
bring some gentleness into this weary world!
Shine on with courageous sensitivity!
You are the light bearers!

133 The Closeness of Happiness

If you are only happy
when others are happy,
you will never be truly happy,
because others do not remain fixed,
but sit in their own power.
Be happy.
Be the container, not the contained;
the source, not the destination.
Allow others to be happy
and allow others to be unhappy,
like so many waves
in your vast ocean,
ever changing.
By leaving others unchanged,
by loving and honoring the place where they are,
you may just change them,
forever.
You may just remind them
of the closeness
of their own happiness.

134   Roots

Friend, I know your heart is broken; I know the future
seems unclear to you; I know you feel the absence of
answers right now; I know you feel a terrible longing for
something you cannot name, but I am here with you.

Let's begin where we are. Let's not focus on the
thousands of steps that will come on the path, but
the place where we stand on the path right now.
And there is only Now!

Know that many others have gone through what
you are going through. Know that sometimes it seems
darkest before the dawn. But instead of longing for
the dawn and rejecting the darkness, let us touch the
dark parts with gentleness and light. Let us meet what
is here, not rush toward what is not yet here. For even
the darkest cave may contain treasure, and even the
most intense and uncomfortable feelings may actually
contain strange medicine.

Walk your path courageously, friend, and know
that your loved ones walk with you.

135 Message from a Dying Friend

I don't want your answers, your good advice. I don't want your theories about "why" or "how." I don't need your pity. Your attempts to make me feel better only make me feel worse. I am human, just like you, and crave realness.

Just be present with me. Listen. Give me space. Hold my trembling hand, sometimes. Your attention is so precious to me. Your being speaks volumes.

If you feel uncomfortable, don't be ashamed. If you don't know what to say to me, that's okay; I feel that way, too, sometimes. If you feel disgusted, angry, uncertain, fearful, that's okay; I love you for it. You are human, too.

Put your textbook learning to one side now. Don't try to have "unconditional positive regard"; it feels so false to me. Forget "empathy"—I want you to come closer than that.

See, I am you, in disguise. These are your broken bones, your shallow breaths, your twisted limbs. I am your mirror; you are seeing yourself.

Don't try to be strong for me. I am not a victim. Fall apart, if you must. Weep, if you need to weep. Mourn those shattered dreams, those lost futures. Let the past slip away, too. Meet me here, now, in the fire of Presence, with the fullness of your being.

I speak in an ancient language now.

I want you to be a witness.

You had no choice. And neither did they.

Instant forgiveness, when you are ready.

Because of what you were going through, how you were feeling at the time, the thoughts that were running through your mind, what you believed then, the lenses through which you were seeing the world, the fear and pain you were grappling with; because of the wounds that had not yet healed, the insights you had not yet had, the information that was missing to you at the time, the horizons that had not yet come into view, the steps you had not yet taken, you had no choice but to act as you acted, say what you said, do what you did, choose as you chose—and neither did they. *You did the best you could, given who you thought you were at the time.* Only in hindsight there seems to have been a choice, and that's exactly what drives us crazy, keeps us lost in guilt and regret.

This is not to condone what happened, of course, or to excuse what happened, nor should this be used to justify any kind of violence. This insight is dedicated to true forgiveness only, in the here and now, to letting go and learning and moving forward, to coming out of the painful and limiting belief that the past could have been any different than it was, and refocusing on the place where real change and reconciliation can happen going forward, your place of true power: the present moment, immediate, alive and complete in itself, no matter what happened in the past.

Acknowledge what happened, learn from your mistakes, grieve over dreams of the way it might have been, recommit to your path in the present; but to imagine things could actually have been any different, is a kind of madness. Bow to the *suchness* of today.

Perhaps it's time to stop trying to "fix" the one in front of you, to stop trying to give them answers or solve their problems. You're not very good at that, friend. Your nature is not manipulation, but presence; not division, but wholeness.

Perhaps it's time to stop pretending to be the all-knowing authority, the infallible teacher, the fully healed expert. Even with the best intentions, you may unknowingly be interfering with their natural healing processes. You may be keeping them dependent on you, distracting them from a deep trust in their own firsthand experience. In trying to fix them, you may just be communicating to them, "you are broken."

Remember, they may need to feel worse before they feel better. They may need to feel their pain *more* deeply before they open up to the true source of healing. They may need to die to who they thought they were, before they can truly live. True for them, true for you.

It's certainly something to consider.

So relax. Breathe. Come out of the drama. Acknowledge your desire to change or fix or even pacify them. Now, simply listen without judgment, and try to understand where they are now. Stand in their shoes. See clearly who and what is in front of you.

Perhaps the greatest help you can offer right now is your clarity and non-judgmental attention, your interest, your understanding, your curiosity. Bring that transmission; be that presence; offer that openness. Stay wide open to solutions that have not yet been born. Be the silent intention—and the right words, actions, interventions, decisions, will come without effort.

Sanctify their moment by not running away. Mirror their own capacity to be present. Trust the ancient mystery of healing.

Perhaps the true medicine can flourish when "you" get out of the way. Yes, drugs and good advice may numb or even silence symptoms, but an invitation to a deeper spiritual healing may be lurking just under the surface.

True Understanding

When a dear friend is in pain, when their sweet and
tender heart is broken wide open, when their world
is spinning out of control, and they don't know
where to turn, sometimes simplicity works wonders.
Often just a simple and genuine "I understand,"
spoken in truth, can be enough—a place to begin.
For you are human, too, and you have known the
pain of heartbreak, you have felt the collapse of
worlds, you have also touched the chaos that lurks
under the surface of things. And so you can say to
your friend, "I hear you. I see you. I am here with
you, now," and just for a moment, you can stand
with them, under-stand them, literally "stand in their
midst," and, just for a moment, you can honor the
place where they stand, even if you don't agree with
their choices. And sometimes, this is where great
healing can begin, the place where you stand together,
the place where you do not stand apart.

How to Sit with Someone Who Longs to Die

When sitting with someone who is suicidal, your naked presence is essential. Don't rush to give them secondhand answers, or tell them they are wrong for thinking their thoughts and feeling their feelings. They would take this as yet another rejection of where they are. They are sick of being manipulated, tired of being told what to do, how to feel, how to live, even how to die. They are desperate for profound connection, for someone to validate them to the very core of their being. They just want to be heard.

Be very aware of your own discomfort, frustration, fear, or sense of powerlessness when sitting with them, and don't assume they feel exactly the same way. Be radically open to their world, their reality, yet take responsibility for your own, too. Stay connected to yourself as you listen. Feel your feet on the ground. Feel your belly rise and fall with each breath. It is essential to take care of yourself.

Remember, as long as they haven't killed themselves yet, they are full of creative potential. Don't focus on what may or may not happen. Don't spout quotes from psychology textbooks or spiritual clichés. Focus on Now. Your mind may be full of nightmarish images of future scenes in their life movie. Remember, this is purely your imagination right now. Stop relating to them as that movie character, the "suicide victim," the picture in your head, and relate to the *one in front of you,* the one who is still here. Be still, here.

They are *alive.* They are here, in your presence. In your fearful mind-movie, they are already gone, but their presence is still shining brightly Now. Deeply connect with the one in front of you, no matter what they say they will do or won't do in the future, no matter how certain they seem, no matter how helpless the situation feels. Stop confusing them with their life story. Their life story is failing, and they seek a way out. But their presence can never fail. Let your presence be their presence. Focus on what is shining.

Remember, they don't really want to end their life, for they *are* life, and will always be. They want to kill the "self"—the mind-made picture of who they are. They want to kill the false identity, the "object"; they want to put an end to who they are not and come alive to who they truly are. They want reunion, to no longer feel "split." They want to live, but just don't know how right now. They want to free themselves from the exhaustion of being a separate self, with its duties and expectations, its pressures and conflicts, its regrets and fears, and rest deeply in the warmth of their own presence. But right now, they see no other way of getting "there" except through physical death.

They have forgotten that "there" is really here. They have forgotten that they are already Home.

Don't invalidate their experience, don't push them even further away from Home, but understand that they are simply misidentified. You can understand their pain—they are a more extreme version of you. They are deeply human. Their pain is real. Bow to it.

They don't want to die—they are desperate to awaken. They want to come alive, to taste life in the way they did when they were very young. Deep down, they know the taste of life, but have forgotten how to taste it. The memory of life haunts them. That's the only reason they want to die—because they know life so very well.

Don't invalidate their urge to die, for at its core is infinite intelligence. Deeply understand their misunderstood longing. Listen to them. Be there for them. Give them space. Offer them the warmth of your unconditional presence. Your touch. Your silent knowing. Your kindness. Meet them in a way that nobody else is able to meet them. Remind them of their infinite worth as an expression of the One Life, their unexplored potential, their true identity beyond the burden of ego.

I have seen astonishing transformations when I have been able to sit with people in this place of profound connection. I understand so well the urge to die—I felt it so many times throughout my teenage years and early adulthood. So many times, I was certain I wouldn't make it. And I also understand that there is another way.

Our story is never set in stone. We all have great potential.

140   Breathe Together

It's easy to teach, to preach, to give memorized answers.
It's easy to be an expert.

It's harder to listen, to really listen.
To be still and wait.
To give someone space.
To receive them with your whole being.

When you think you know what's "best" for someone,
when you're excited by your own vision,
when you want to jump in with great advice,
take a deep breath.
Slow down.
Trust.

Your friend may not need what's "best" right now.
They may just need *you*.

Kinship can be the most potent medicine.

Sometimes true answers emerge
when questions are allowed to breathe.

141   For This and This Alone

If ever there was any proof that only love mattered, if proof was ever needed, then witness the falling away of time as your ninety-year-old mother dies in your arms. It is almost a birth, an unspeakable intimacy, some kind of insurrection against all the supposed forces of darkness. It was only yesterday that she held you in her arms as you hold her now. And where did all the time go? The light is almost unbearable.

Dive into it, friend. Let it break you open.

See, we shall not be individuals, we shall not be alone, but part of something vast and incomprehensible. Mother returns to womb, to simplicity, and a tiny robin chirps his first song of newness and heartache in the garden outside the hospital room, the final room, the temple.

Give your life to opening.

142   Note to a Recovering Friend

Your illness is not against you. The aches and pains you feel in your body are not punishments. You did nothing wrong. You are not broken in spirit, even in the midst of this discomfort. *The way things are* is *the way things should be.* You are receiving yet another invitation today—to slow down. To rest. To stay close to yourself in these challenging times. To take each moment as it comes. To meet life on its own terms. To let go of all that which is unnecessary, including perhaps your search for answers, reasons, solutions. To reassess your priorities, to remember That Which Is Primary. To turn toward the present moment, this moment, the only moment there is, your true Home, your resting place, your place of connection.

To stay rooted here, in the present scene of the movie of your life. To stop rewinding the movie into past scenes of regret, missed chances, and wrong turns. And to stop fast-forwarding the movie into future scenes of pain or sorrow, further missed chances, unattainable goals, or even death. To come right back here. To befriend uncertainty, rediscover the thrill of not knowing. To say "yes!" to this moment, even if you feel like a "no." *To include the "no," too; it is also one of your children.*

To use your aches and pains, not be used by them; to meet the sensations in your body with gentleness and curiosity, not to resist them or try to make them go away. To sink deeply into the moment; not to try to escape it—and to allow yourself to want to escape it, too, sometimes. To trust the intelligence of this incredible body, its extraordinary capacity to heal and deal with anything that comes its way. To admit that you are exhausted from the struggle of pretending to be a "me," tired from trying to fit in, trying to say the right thing, trying to be a success in the world, trying to hold it all together, even trying not to try. You long for rest. Give yourself rest.

Drop the word "sick," let go of the words "ill" and "broken" and "damaged"; see this as a path of deeper healing, beyond the physical. A calling to Truth. Always a beginning, never a defeat.

143 To a Friend Who Has Loved and Lost

Your precious heart is raw and bleeding now, friend, and no words can comfort you. But I want you to know, I am here with you. My heart breaks with yours. You are not alone in this ancient place.

Because you loved her and love her still, even at her passing, you are willing to feel the pain of loss now, the sorrow, the grief, the shock. You are feeling nothing less than the breaking open of your dreams, yesterday's dreams of tomorrow's joys shattering into light and shade. A new world is emerging.

Let it all move through, today; don't resist the breaking, honor it even, bow to it. Remember, your loved one cannot truly die. Only the body is dropped, only the physical, only everything she was not. So in that way she is still with you, in love; for in love, as love, you are always connected, and not even death has power to change that.

But knowing that intellectually is not enough. Grieve the change of form today, your shattered dream, her newfound freedom. Don't try to feel "happy." Happiness is a lie to you right now. Don't rush toward healing, or even "feeling better." It will all come, in time; tomorrow will take care of you. Today is a day to

honor the sorrow and uncertainty you feel now, to feel
the power of life in the feelings you feel, not to have
all your questions answered, or to skip to the scene of
"being okay" or "moving on." *It's okay not to feel okay
right now.*

Our hearts are with you now, all of us throughout
history who have loved and lost and let go of illusions.
We are many. This is an ancient rite of passage, not
a mistake or a punishment, although right now you
don't need to understand any of this.

Just cry. Scream. Wail. Fall to your knees. You
are held by the ground as you meet her, and yourself,
more deeply than ever. Death has no power over
your love!

Turn Your Light Way Up

When someone calls you names, reduces you to
a thing, when they offer advice you didn't ask for,
when they blame you for their pain, when they do
not listen to you, and endlessly talk about themselves,
when they compare you with others, when they
ignore, invalidate, judge or ridicule your thoughts
and feelings . . .

Stop. Breathe. Feel your feet in contact with the
sacred Earth. Feel the safety of the moment.

Know it's their pain, not yours. Know they are
dreaming the only dream they can dream until they
wake up. Know that they don't know the real you,
only their fantasy.

Perhaps they find it hard to love themselves.
Perhaps they seek their worth externally. Perhaps
they are disconnected from their breath, their bodies,
their precious aliveness, their true calling, their path.
Perhaps they live in a dualistic world of good and
bad, right and wrong, success and failure. Perhaps
they have forgotten the simple joy of being.

Perhaps you understand this. Perhaps you have
been where they have been.

Don't try to change them now. They may never
change. Don't try to fix them. They aren't asking to
be fixed right now, obviously. The more you push,
they more they'll push back.

Don't get entangled in their web of sorrows. See clearly, have compassion, but don't push.

It's okay that they are upset. It really is. Give them space to be upset. It's okay that they are disappointed in you. Give them space to be disappointed. It's okay that they judge you. Make room for their judgments, too.

Make room for your own thoughts and feelings! Allow yourself to feel sad, angry, guilty, doubtful. Let all these precious energies wash through you. They will not harm you, when you allow them to move. Don't blame the other person for your feelings; hold your feelings close, they are your children.

Yes, you will meet many gatekeepers on this journey, many naysayers, many judges. Walk your path anyway, and allow others to walk theirs. You don't need to justify your path or defend it. Nobody can stop you from walking it.

Stay close to yourself in these challenging times. Do not fight the darkness; it has no power anyway. Simply turn your light up, way up.

145 A New Dawn

You cannot save anyone. You can be present with
them, offer your groundedness, your sanity, your
peace. You can even share your path with them, offer
your perspective. But you cannot take away their pain.
You cannot walk their path for them. You cannot give
answers that are right for them, or even answers they
can digest right now. They will have to find their own
answers, ask their own questions or lose their own
questions, make friends with their own uncertainty.
They will need to make their own mistakes, feel their
own sorrows, learn their own lessons. If they truly
want to be at peace, they will have to trust the path of
healing that reveals itself step-by-step. But you cannot
heal them. You cannot diffuse their fear, their anger,
their feelings of powerlessness. You cannot save them,
or make things right for them. If you push too hard,
they may lose their own unique way. Your way may
not be their way, however much that possibility hurts
or confuses you now.

You did not create their pain. You may have
done or not done some things, said or not said some
things, triggering pain that was already inside them.
But you did not create it, and you are not guilty,
even if they say you are. You can take responsibility
for your words and deeds, yes, you can grieve over
a past, and you can even say sorry and mean it, but
you cannot erase or change what happened, and you

cannot control the future. You can only meet them in the here and now, your place of power. You are not responsible for their happiness, and they are not responsible for yours.

Your happiness cannot come from outside of you. If it does, it is a dependent happiness, a fragile happiness that will turn to sorrow so quickly. And then you will get caught up in a web of blame and guilt, regret and persecution. Your happiness is directly related to your presence, your connection with your breath, your body, the earth. Your happiness is not small, and cannot be removed by fear, or anger, or the most intense shame. Your happiness is not a state, or a passing experience, or even a feeling that others can give to you. Your happiness is vast, ever-present, the boundless space of the heart, in which joy and sorrow, bliss and boredom, certainty and doubt, loneliness and connection, even fear and longing, can move like the weather, like the rain and the sunshine, all held in the hugeness of the sky.

You cannot save anyone, and you cannot be saved if you are looking to be saved. There is no self to save, no self to lose, no self to defend, no self to make perfect or perfectly happy. Let go of every impossible ideal. You are beautiful in your imperfection, outrageously perfect in your doubts, lovable even in your feelings of unloveability. All these parts have been given, all are parts of the whole, and you were never less than whole.

You are breathing. You know you are alive. You have a right to exist, feel what you feel, think what you think, speak your truth even if your voice shakes. You have a right to your joy and a right to your sorrows. You have a right to doubt, too. You have a right to walk your path. You have a right to be right and a right to be wrong, a right to this giant happiness that you knew when you were young. You are breathing, and you are inseparable from the life force that animates all things, knows itself as all beings, discovers itself in every moment of this impossibly wondrous existence.

Your self-worth is not tied to what others think of you. It is tied to the moon, to the infinite expanse of the cosmos, to comets blazing toward unknown destinations, to the forgetting of time and the love of solitude and this unspeakable gratitude for each new morning, unexpected, given.

Walk Your Path with Courage!

When someone criticizes or judges you, please remember, they are only criticizing or judging a part of their own heart, a reflection of themselves in you. We are all mirrors to each other. Don't take their attack personally. They do not know the real you, only an image. And if you believe they should think or feel differently right now, if you don't want them to have the experience they're having, you are lost in a fantasy, too. Allow them their opinion, and allow yourself yours. Feel your feelings, think your thoughts; and know that people are only "right" from their own perspective.

If someone thinks you are bad or wrong, it doesn't mean that you *are* bad or wrong. Don't internalize their criticism or judgment; let *them* believe what they believe. And perhaps—if they are willing to listen and self-reflect—help them understand more clearly your experience, your voice, your heart, and listen to theirs. You have nothing to defend, because the truth is the truth, and the truth will out. There is no need to take things personally, and if you do take things personally, you are still not bad or wrong, only human, and wonderful in your humanness. It can be both terrifying and thrilling to realize that everybody is dreaming of you until they wake, and they wake only when they wake. And perhaps they never wake.

So walk your path with courage, knowing there will always be those who advise you to turn back and go home. Thank them for their opinion and keep walking; your heart yearns for the Unknown, and pumps for the thrill of an original path forging itself with each new day; do not apologize for your love of life, your torrid affair with the Mystery.

And with every judgment, with every criticism, you see more clearly.

PART XII **Rest in the Wholeness of Life**

147   You!

What is Presence? Presence is the felt sense of being alive, of existing, here and now. The living field of *I Am* that has never come or gone, of which even *I Am* is already a translation by mind.

Thoughts, sensations, feelings, sounds, smells, all kinds of states and experiences both mundane and profound, have all come and gone in your life, but your Presence has never come or gone, appeared or disappeared. The silent unchanging backdrop to all experience, the vast ocean of You, constant and steady amidst all the arising and dissolving of the waves of the manifest world.

You, in the most intimate sense of the word. You, as you have always known yourself, closer than breathing. The You that was present when you took your first breath, that will be present when you take your last breath, that is present on every in-breath and every out-breath.

Present as you took your first steps, present as you take your last. Present on your first day of school, your wedding day, and as you held your grandfather's hand for the last time. You, prior to even the word "you." Unknowable by thought, unable to be conceptualized, and yet the one thing you've always known more deeply that you've known anything. The one undoubtable thing; the one thing you've never been able to put into words; the one thing that's always been on the tip of your tongue; the one thing that's not a "thing" at all.

The You that you recognize in everyone you meet. The condition by which you've known anything at all. Undoubtable, since even doubt is allowed to come and go.

That which you have always sought, that which has been present throughout all your seeking and suffering and longing for union.

Your true Home, your most profound sense of rest, your beloved; it was always You.

148   Coming Out

I am gay.

I am straight.

I am lesbian, bisexual, transsexual, transgender. I am a man, I am a woman, and everything in between. I am a Christian, a Jew, a Hindu, a Buddhist, a Muslim, a Sikh, a humanist, a pagan, a Satanist. I am an agnostic, an atheist, a nihilist, a dualist and a non-dualist, a believer and a non-believer, a somebody and a nobody.

I am the space for laughter, tears, agony and ecstasy, the most ecstatic bliss and the most profound heartbreak, despair and disillusionment. I am the space for the wonderful dreams, the terrible nightmares, memories, visions, and the most creative manifestations of light. All thoughts, all stories, all concepts, all sensations, all possible feelings, human and animal, vegetable and mineral, pass through me, arise out of me, and fall back into me.

I am Consciousness itself. I am what you are.

I am coming out as Love.

149   The Guru

The one who makes you laugh until your stomach
hurts and you snort like a pig is your guru.
The one who brings tears to your eyes, the one who
makes you weep your secrets out is your guru.
The one who challenges you, triggers old pain in you,
makes you face your deepest fears and longings,
helps you tell the truth is your guru.
Every breath is your guru. Every beat of the heart.
Every sound.
The morning breeze caressing your cheek is your guru.
The car that won't stop, the missed opportunity, the
broken promise, the shattered bone, these are all
your gurus.
The ones you love, the ones who frustrate you like
anything, the ones who bore you to tears, the
ones you don't want to remember, the ones who
left, they are your gurus, too.
This entire life, so fleeting, so present, so rich with
blessings, is your guru.
You can seek your guru in an ashram, a church, a
temple, a science lab; you can search for salvation
in a cave on a mountaintop in India; but, friend, if
you look deeply into the present, you will find you
are already there. The true altar is where you stand;
the holy book writes itself moment by moment.
The Kingdom is spread out over the Earth, waiting
for open eyes.

150　How to Rebirth Yourself

When you were a little one, you were a ball of pure creativity, an explosion of raw and ancient energies, energies you had no way of naming, let alone understanding, let alone integrating.

Unnamed joys and sorrows surged through you without warning, prehistoric longings, rages, undigested terrors—the snake, the velociraptor, the unnameable movement in the deep, watching, waiting. The overwhelming feeling of being alive, tasting your own taste, being in your own being, moving as a body. You were a riot of light and sound, an amorphous mass of pure sensation, often startled and overjoyed in equal measure, out of time and out of control, out of the safety of the womb, outside of Mother, and your very life was at stake in every moment, or so it seemed.

You are essentially no different now. Yet you have been taught how to be a good boy or girl, kind, polite, careful, consistent, nice, right, even "spiritual." You have been taught the right things to say, to want, to ask, to seek, to feel, to think, to do.

Know your place. Don't ask too much. Stay small. Don't stray too far from the herd. You have become civilized, taught to push away half of your nature. Brainwashed, even, to believe that half—or more—of your being is sinful, sick, bad, broken, evil, dark, unenlightened, unawakened, unspiritual, negative, untrustable, pathological, unintelligent, damaged.

Don't feel sad, they say. Don't feel angry. Don't feel fear. Don't doubt. Don't talk back. Don't have negative thoughts. Don't be in a low vibration. Don't wallow. Pretend to be something you are not. Conform. Be like us. Heal. Don't question. Don't trust yourself. Get enlightened. It goes on and on.

You have split yourself in two in the name of love and freedom. And it was so intelligent to do so. You were only seeking safety and sense in a world that often made no sense, looking for sanity amidst a cacophony of nonsense. Your defenses were creative, not pathological . . .

"Shut up baby, stop crying! Cry, baby, why won't you cry? Why do you want so much? Don't touch that. Stand, don't stand. Walk, sit still. Behave! Why are you just sitting there? Bad child. Good child. Bad child. Don't be such a child! Do something! Stop it! I love you. I'll only love you if you . . . I love you. I hate you. Speak up! Shut up! You just ate. Go to your room. Eat! Why are you still in your room? How dare you say that! Shh, baby. Baby? Why are you so quiet? I'm here for you. I'm not here for you. I might be here for you. You're bad. You're sick. You're good. You're nice. You're evil. You're perfect. You don't need me. You need me. I need you to need me. You are so needy! Grow up! Get over it. Get over here! Leave me alone! Come back!"

It made no sense.

How to navigate it all without getting hurt? How to please Mummy or Daddy? How to hold it all?

Am I loved? Is it safe? When will they leave me alone? Why have they abandoned me? Do they see? Is there something wrong with me? Am I broken? Are they broken? Am I whole or half or less? Do I exist? Is this my life? Can I trust myself? Should I trust them? Can I trust my lack of trust? Why can't I trust? What's wrong with me? Should I talk or not talk? Stay or go? Feel or not feel? Smile or not smile? Laugh or cry? Run or sit still? Go forward or backward? Tell the truth? Lie to protect myself? To protect them? Let it out? Hold it in? What if they find out what I really think? Can they see into me? Am I being watched? Is something rotting inside me? Should I stand or fight? Change or stagnate? Whose path am I on? Will it always be like this? What did I do wrong? What did I do right? Do I deserve this? Who do they think I am?

Friend, you are grown now, and it is time to question your basic fear of life, your fearful programming; to unlearn what you learned when you were a little one and you craved love and life, and to begin to realize that love is not something given but something lived, something deep and ancient and trustworthy within you, and you are not sick, or wrong, or bad, or evil, or unworthy, or crazy, or damaged beyond repair, or a freak of nature; but you are so damn alive, nature itself, an explosion of creativity, an amorphous and intelligent mass of ancient energies that you need not understand, or escape, or numb yourself to, but hold in your vast heart, and breathe into, and trust.

You are no longer a little one, but a vast One, as you always were, despite your growing body, a wide-open space in which all these energies that you once pushed away and disowned can now celebrate themselves, dance as waves in your oceanic embrace, and self-liberate.

In a sea of non-duality (non-separation), a Oneness that you are, all thoughts, sounds, sensations are not *against* life, but *are* life; not mistakes or punishments or signs of your failure, not separate from you, but little celebrations of you, beloved waves in the ocean, embraceable. Or rather, they are already embraced, for they are timeless, not yours yet intimately yours, as the clouds do not belong to the sky but dance within it.

There is nothing you have to do to receive this grace. It is not a state, not something you can reach, attain, or be given. It cannot be transmitted by gurus in loincloths. It is not a reward for your spiritual or material success. It is already here, shining within your very ordinary experience.

In the beginning you were a child of human parents, but now you are your own parent, that ever-present awareness shining on all movements within and without, that undying Presence by which you know you are loved, always, even when you get it all wrong, even when you stumble and fall and doubt, even when you are hungry and tired and don't know where to turn.

You are loved for you are Love, the lover and the beloved as One.

I am here with you, child, it says. *I am here. You are the One, my chosen One. Even when you feel alone and far from love, I am here. Trust this moment. Trust this ground. This breath. This devastation. This birth, this loss of your old world. Trust, even if you feel you cannot trust. Trust that, too. I am here with you, closer than this next exhale.*

And its voice is your voice, your heart its heart, and the world is its womb, and you are forever born anew in each moment, thrust into life, bruised and gasping but alive, exhausted but alive, and you breathe with every living being, and nobody can ever take this love away from you now, nobody can break your spirit.

You are so damn worthy of life.

I teach this, and only this: an unconditional love more timeless than the stars.

151   Beyond the Mask

Never come to a conclusion about anyone.
They will always surprise you.
For they are alive, and ever changing,
with no fixed "self" to call their own.

They are a cast of thousands.
Shape-shifters. A parade of masks.
Tragic, comic, fierce, ecstatic, numb.
Do not confuse them with their appearance!
See the Universal Self underneath.

Breathe. Stay open.
You will be humbled.

152   The Presence

If you cannot feel God's presence,
then feel your own presence
and know it as God.

If you cannot find love,
it is because you are seeking it
in time and in space.

If you do not know your path,
it is because you are already walking it
(fearlessly, and without a map).

If you cannot reach the answers now,
it is because you are embracing the questions
(answers come in their own sweet time).

When you feel far away from God,
when Home seems like a distant memory,
you are closer than you could possibly imagine.

So breathe, and love the next step.

153

Understanding the Urge to Die

I spent the first half of my life wanting to die. And here is what I discovered: *the urge to die is the urge to live, ingeniously disguised.*

The urge to die is the urge to disappear as a separate self, to vanish into the vastness of Being, to rest deeply in our true nature. It is the wave longing to return to the ocean . . . forgetting that it was never divided from the ocean in the first place. An innocent mistake, easily corrected with a little investigation.

The urge to die is not negative, crazy, sick, dark, or sinful, but it is deeply, deeply misunderstood, that's for sure! We ignore the urge, push it away, hide it, medicate it, keep it a secret, shame it, try to numb ourselves to it, or even philosophize it away. But when acknowledged, honored, listened to, even the suicidal urge, the urge to shed our false skin, contains infinite intelligence. All feelings do!

Secretly, the urge to die is the urge to awaken, to come alive, to stop identifying as a separate body-mind, to remember our original nature, vast and free! It is the urge to shed the false "me" (ego, self, person), to stop pretending to be something we are not, to let go of all that is secondhand and inauthentic, and to live, to really live, fearless and free, as Consciousness itself, full of life and potential and cosmic creativity!

The urge to die is not our enemy—it is not to be annihilated and not to be feared. It contains a profound message of awakening and change. It says, shouts, screams, "You are not limited to what you think you are! You are a child of the universe, remember, deserving of all its riches! Only the false can die, and you cannot be false!" Can we hear its call? Can we listen, really listen?

The wave cannot return to the ocean, cannot get Home. It was never divided from its Home in the first place! You are already oceanic, friend, and the true suicide is not the stopping of the body-mind, but the remembrance of your original and unblemished nature, here and now, beyond the ravages of time!

Live! Live! Live! Nothing to lose!

154

A Yogi of Broken Dreams

Don't worship a bearded old man in the sky or a
graven image in a book. Worship the in-breath and the
out-breath, the winter breeze caressing your face,
the morning rush on the subway, the simple feeling
of being alive, never knowing what is to come. See
God in the eyes of a stranger, Heaven in the broken
and the ordinary. Worship the ground on which you
stand. Make each day a dance, with tears in your eyes
as you behold the divine in every moment, see the
absolute in all things relative, and let them call you
crazy. Let them laugh and point. You are a yogi of
traffic jams and discarded apple cores, aloneness and
impossibly blue winter skies, a yogi of broken dreams,
mad with truth and devotion and inexplicable joy,
and you cannot be saved now.

155   A New Spirituality

We'd like to introduce ourselves:
We are a new generation of spiritual inquirers.
We no longer require secondhand answers.
We no longer blame others for our suffering.
Our spirituality goes beyond cosmic guilt
    and punishment
and "us and them" thinking.
We no longer cling to holy books,
for all books are holy.
We don't kill over truth,
for truth is all around.
We are willing to fearlessly face present experience
without conclusions and without prejudice,
naked as the day we were born,
open to what comes.

We are no longer waiting for life
or some divine revelation in the future,
for we see life in everything,
including the waiting for life
and God in all that we once rejected.

We no longer dream of escape
or some perfect "Heaven,"
for we have relaxed into uncertainty,
and doubt is an old friend,
and not-knowing is dearly beloved,
and imperfection is deeply holy to us.

The body is included.
Mind is not the enemy.
Feelings are sacred.
Sexuality is celebrated.
We love the mess of being human!

And we finally understand
that wisdom and compassion,
absolute and relative,
duality and non-duality,
transcendence and immanence,
personal and impersonal,
human and divine,
were never divided at all.

Rays of Sunshine
through the Clouds

In the midst of conflict,
have you ever suddenly felt a near-unbearable wave
   of compassion
for the one on the "other side"?

Has your "enemy" suddenly and without warning
   become . . . closer?

You are not crazy. You are not "going soft."
You are waking up.

You have felt their pain as your own, their struggle as
   your struggle.
You have forgotten all your clever reasons to be at war.
You have lost interest in winning.
You have remembered that once you were kin.
In another life, perhaps, or in another reality, or in
   another moment,
they were your brother, your sister, your mother, your
   friend, your son.

Once, you held them in your arms so tenderly.
Once, you played together in the river.

Perhaps you will play again.

Perhaps you are the hope of this world.

Your Outrageous Fire

Don't define yourself, friend. Definitions are dead, of the past—and you are so alive!

You're not a good person or a bad person. You're not a wise person or a fool. You're not a success or a failure. You're not beautiful, nor are you ugly. You're not a relaxed person or a stressful person. You're not enlightened, and you can't be unenlightened, ever. You're not any one thing, nor many things at once. You are pure potential. Openness. A vessel for life, prior to any incarnation as "this kind of person" or "that kind of person." You are alive.

No concept can capture your vastness. No mouth can speak your name. No word can capture your outrageous fire. You cannot define yourself; all definitions are too late.

You always knew you were changing too fast to be pinned down.

158   Why You Want to Die Sometimes

If you ever feel like taking your own life, if you ever feel a longing to die, if the thought *I want to kill myself* comes to visit, do not fear and do not despair. Celebrate that a deep intelligence is at work in you. Know that it's the most natural thing in the world to want to die, a rite of passage, a misunderstood calling. It is not a sin, not wrong, not a sign of your weakness or failure, not a symptom of a terrible disease or darkness inside you. You are not mad, not damaged, not unworthy of life, not "bad." The urge to leave is an urge as old as the universe itself, something all human beings have known in some form or other. Know that you are not alone, but connected to all humanity in your aloneness.

The urge to die doesn't need to be followed or indulged, but understood; not numbed away or acted upon, *but embraced for what it is*. Translated, "I want to die" means "I feel homesick, and I desperately want to go Home, but don't know *how* right now." The urge to die is the natural urge to shed the illusion of the separate self, to let go of the exhausting burden of "me and my life" (who you are not) and rest deeply in Presence (who you are). It is a call to remember your true Home beyond all earthly homes—here and now. To taste your own taste once again. To come out of the story of past and future and live in this precious moment. To be here, fearlessly present, courageously alive, no longer at war with the pain and bliss of life, no longer resisting the slings and arrows of existence.

Use the thought *I want to die* to begin a deep meditation on the nature of self. Who will die? Who would want to kill a "self"? Who lives now? Who breathes? If the "self" can be killed, if it can be loved or hated, is it really who you are? What is the intelligence in you that knows that the "self" is impermanent and can be lost? Is that intelligence not fully present and alive and awake now? The "successful self" and the "failed self," the "wonderful self" and the "terrible self," the "self that wants to die" and the "self that wants to live," are these not all images, pictures, ideas, movies, floating in your eternal movie screen presence right now? Are you not beyond all of these concepts? Are you not the space for it all?

If you have taken "self" to mean less than who you truly are, of course you want to "end" it, for it feels too small in your vastness. If you know your "self" as Self, your own presence beyond birth and death, then you cannot really kill yourself, for presence cannot kill presence, just as the ocean cannot kill the ocean, and the sun cannot stop shining, even though it burns.

You are tired, friend. You feel burnt out. You shine so brightly. You long for Home. So rest, and know that your longing to die is not a mistake but an expression of great intelligence, reminding you of your deep love of life, your unlimited nature, and your cosmic innocence.

You are Home, already. A new life is dawning for you. Stay open. There will be unexpected gifts, I promise. And I speak as one who wanted to die for many years.

159   Whatever You Dream

Accepting where you are in life, being present to what is immediate and alive, falling in love with the here and now, is *not* the same as giving up on the possibility of future change. Quite the opposite.

Please, do not stop dreaming those beautiful dreams, imagining a future for yourself and the world that makes your heart sing.

But, in the midst of dreams, do not forget That Which Never Dreams, the wide-open space that holds it all. Do not lose touch with your true nature, already complete, forever whole, in need of nothing, profoundly connected to all there is. Do not forget this moment in your pursuit of "what's next."

It is from this moment, from a place of profound connection and rest that your new life will grow. Being present does not mean deleting or denying the possibility of past and future, it means remembering your true ground, wherever you are, whatever you dream.

It is from the canvas of the present moment that all your tomorrows will be painted. You can't paint on tomorrow's canvas, for tomorrow never comes. Only today, only today—and that is the gorgeous paradox of awakening.

Dream and, simultaneously, let go of those dreams, without contradiction; and be here. For in this dreamworld, anything is possible.

There but for the Grace of God

Even the homeless guy on the street is of noble birth and outrageous inheritance.

When you look into his bloodshot eyes, you see godly things and potential beyond comprehension, even if he himself has forgotten. To see anything less in him is sheer certifiable insanity.

You are only ever seeing aspects of your original Face, friend. Ever since you were a child, you always knew that the separate "I" was the greatest illusion of all.

161 The Constant Teacher

You have never been without a teacher, not for one moment. Throughout the joys and the sorrows; throughout the visions, the visits to transcendent realms, the astral travel, the ecstatic journeys, the waking, dreaming, and deep sleeping states; throughout the times of great release and the times you thought you'd never make it, your teacher was Presence, and Presence was always You.

Think of how much of your pain lives in the past, friend, and how little by comparison lives in the present. Think of all the fears that never materialized, the nightmares that remained nightmares, the imagined tomorrows that dissolved into today's laughter or tears.

Know that your yesterdays and tomorrows are always melting into today's presence, today's new breaths, and honor the place where you breathe.

Remember that love is not a feeling that comes and goes, nor a state that approaches and recedes, nor the vague memory of something long gone, nor something that can be given and taken away, but a recognition that we are all the same Life, the same Mystery, looking out of unique eyes, yet knowing the same shock and pulse and hum of existence.

162 Love Is Stronger Than Death

Where does a loved one "go" when they die?
Where does a wave "go" when it crashes onto
    the shore?
Nowhere. No place.

The wave was never separate from the ocean in the
    first place, so it cannot "return" there. Water
    cannot leave water, nor can it go back.
Nothing happens at all, from the perspective of our
    true nature.
Death is simply the deepest relaxation into our
    unborn, undying presence.

Your loved one did not "go" anywhere, friend. They
    simply rested even more deeply in their own
    nature, which is your nature, which is Presence.
    Not two. Never two.
They are now where they always were—in your heart
    of hearts. And they can never leave.

You will carry them.
Love is stronger than death.

163 You Do Not Breathe Alone

When you were a fetus, you could not breathe by yourself. So Mother breathed for you.

Her breath was your breath. Her blood was your blood. Her life was yours.

There was a tiny hole in your heart called the "foramen ovale." Most likely, it closed at birth, when you took your first breath.

You screamed. You wailed. You were in shock. You were bruised, perhaps. Sore, swollen, bloody, tiny, you wept for your existence, grieved the loss of a womb-world.

You were exhausted, but you were alive.

So you knew early on that life was not all bliss and ecstasy. It was pain, too. It was overwhelm. It was loss of the womb.

But in the overwhelm, beauty. And in the loss, love. And hope. And discovery.

Friend, sometimes you need to cry, and splutter, and scream, and make a mess, and forget the future, and old worlds.

And come to rejoice in a single breath.

And the joyous beating of a holy heart.

To this day, you do not breathe alone.

164   The Root of All Desire

At the root of every desire is the desire for ourselves.

We tend to believe that something external—a person, an object, a substance, a certain pleasurable or intense experience—can satisfy our desires. Secretly, what we desire, of course, is that sense of relief, rest, satisfaction, *home,* which comes from a desire being fulfilled, satiated. For when we finally get what we want, or what we thought we wanted, we can finally relax; we are no longer in want, no longer caught up in the discomfort of lack. We are, finally, present to ourselves, no longer seeking outside ourselves for satisfaction, but feeling the satisfaction inherent in our own presence, that sense of cosmic rightness, of being at home, of no longer needing anything external to complete ourselves.

We are no longer split in two, as the "one who desires" over here, divided in time and space from the "desired one" over there, but whole, at rest, content, One. The burning over, we rest in our own nature, temporarily; a brief respite from desire.

But as we all know, the satisfaction doesn't last for long. It is an illusion that desire could ever end desire. The system simply reboots, and a new desire burns, and a new search for relief, and so on, and so on, world without end.

And so allow desire, first directed outward into time and space, projected onto objects and people and places, to turn back into itself, fall into its own Source. Come to know desire more intimately, as a longing for Presence, for Home.

All desire is really for the Self. So do not try to numb or extinguish all desires (self-mortification), or seek the end of desire through trying to satisfy every conceivable desire (self-indulgence), but embrace desire for what it is, embrace it fully in the present moment, and simply decouple it from the "content," the narrative, the future, the story. Honor the burning in the belly, chest, throat, feel the raw sensations there, without judging them, labeling them, or trying to make them stop. Feel the burning of life itself. And let the burning be embraced. Be the home for it. See the desire as a lost child burning for love, begging to be included, not extinguished; held, not healed; accepted, not abandoned.

You are burning for yourself, friend, and, when you stop to take a look, you are never actually far away. You are closer than any object, any person, any substance, any experience. This is true full-fillment; being *full* of breath, *filled* with life, close to yourself. Forever One with what you always desired.

Let every desire guide you back to the source of all desires—You.

165 This Pull toward Home

Sometimes the path is badly lit. We stumble over
ourselves in the dark. All tangled limbs, flailing.
Hands reaching out to grab us.

Strange things there, unnameable, lonely, longing.
Stay close to me, my love. Keep hold of my hand.
No, I do not know the way! Yes, I am as lost
as you are! But I feel . . . I feel this love. I cannot
explain it.

There is a light in the darkness! There is a call of
the heart, I have felt it for years. It is my only guide,
this yearning. This pull toward Home.

We are lost, yes, but we are held. Beckoned by
something ancient.

Stay close to me. Breathe, my love.

I will not leave you here.

166 I Am

The ocean is not absent, even in the smallest wave. And in the largest wave, the ocean is perfectly present.

Your presence, that unchanging sense of *I Am,* that simple, intimate feeling of being alive, here and now, that nobody had to teach you, that needs no proof, no external validation, that you intuitively know as your deepest sense of identity, and dignity, and power, is never absent, even in the midst of terror, rage, despair, the most profound doubt, waves of grief, shame. It cannot abandon you. No experience can destroy it. And every thought, sound, sensation, dream, memory, arises and falls in its boundless and indestructible embrace.

It is the Source. It is there in the silence and in the noise. It is there in the chaos and in the calm. It is there even in the looking.

It is closer than the next breath. (It breathes with you, as you.)

It is not an object, a form, a definable "thing," yet it takes shape as all things, dances as worlds.

And when you feel lost, you are already found here. And when you doubt, there is great certainty here. And when you cannot hold yourself, you are held here. And when you feel far from love, even that is beloved, here.

It is what you are. It is life itself, unbreakable, free.

It is the living root of every thought, sensation, dream. It cannot be understood, yet is there even in confusion.

In a million different ways, you have only ever been seeking yourself.

PART XIII

Rest in the Journey, Not the Destination

167   The Call of the Warrior

Do not follow anyone. Listen, take what you take,
but do not follow. When you follow someone,
you begin to fear yourself. Following keeps you
dependent, always looking outward. And your
leaders may be themselves blind.

Leave the path prescribed for you. Drop the map.
It was always someone else's map.

You feel rejected? Then feel rejected. You feel like
an outcast? Then feel like an outcast. You feel alone?
So feel alone. Dive into that aloneness. Explore its
depths. Follow its sacred rhythms; see where it leads.
Follow the breath as it rises and falls. Follow your
feet as they meet the ground. Follow the dance of
sensation in your body.

In silence, you may at last be able to hear it: the
wild call of the heart. The power in your aloneness.
This unbreakable connection to earth.

Your path may be challenging; your calling
is strong.

Suddenly, for whatever reason, while walking down
a familiar path, you notice that the destination has
become more important than the journey itself. Your
urgency to reach the goal has pushed every precious
step out of focus. You have been walking blindly,
unconsciously, not really present to your walk,
mesmerized by a future, disconnected and alone,
walking down a familiar path.

The focus then shifts, from the imagined future
scene of the movie of your life, to the present scene,
here, now. From what is not present to what is
present. You feel your living body again, the
thumping of your heart, the breath going in and
out, the softness of the ground underneath your
feet, the gentle breeze on your face; you hear the
rustling of trees all around and the barking of
dogs in the distance. You feel supported, again,
connected to everything and everyone. Life has
been exploding everywhere, but you were focused
elsewhere, in some other time and place. You notice
tension and tiredness all over your body, tightness
in your shoulders and chest. You forgive yourself for
neglecting yourself. You bring warm, loving presence
to these neglected parts, and this allows the tension

to relax and dissolve in its own time. You are relieved to be Home again, present to your walk. Your hopes and fears about the future pale in comparison to this immediacy, this aliveness.

You will get to your destination, perhaps. But right now, the walk is everything. Every step is reminding you how to live. Every breath is a little guru.

169   You Are Wild Now

Sometimes you are walking alone, and it is late,
and you are lost once again in the dream of past and
future, of yesterdays lost and tomorrows unlived,
of choices to be made or not made, of words to be
spoken or left unspoken. Yesterday's enlightenment
feels a million miles away, and the spiritual clarity
you thought you had has faded into the evening.
Now, there is only the sound of footsteps on a
cold pavement, the rustling of trees before sleep,
the naked glow of orange streetlamps, and a deep
melancholy burning inside. You are out of time,
out of body, finding your home in neither form
nor the formless. Perhaps you are the only one of
your species on the planet. Perhaps you do not even
exist at all. Perhaps this is the price you pay for
awakening, for your commitment to opening your
heart to everything, this never-ceasing questioning of
everything solid, this abandonment of every single
reference point.

And suddenly you remember: *this too is life!*
For whatever reason, you turn toward your present
experience, you hold it again the way a mother holds
her newborn baby. You focus on what you have, not
what you have lost; what you see, not what you may
never see again. Your solitude is sacred, you remember,

your doubts are nothing less than holy, the evening breeze on your cheeks is a caress, a kiss, not a block to some imagined future.

It is okay to feel the way you feel. It is okay to feel a little broken by life. It is okay to touch the depths in yourself. It is okay to forget, and to remember, to remember, and to forget. All movements are held in the vastness, as the ground holds the trees, as the sky holds the planet, as the house holds the family, as the story of your life is held in pristine awareness on this night of all nights. Even your disconnection is so damn connected. There is something humbling about never being able to come to a conclusion, something touching in your raw vulnerability to the evening, the way you are moved by everything now, your sensitivity to even the subtlest movement of consciousness, your heart that cannot be closed.

You vow to never lose your love for these evenings. They have brought you so much.

Presence is not a destination, friend, it is the ground. You are wild now, and unbound.

Turn Back, Right Now!

If you want to "feel good" all the time,
please, forget about waking up.

If you want to wake up,
forget about "feeling good."

If you long for the raw truth of existence,
please, prepare for the shattering of your status quos.
Prepare for heartbreak, the devastation of dreams.

Everything you know about yourself
will be smashed into a million pieces.

Prepare to allow an unimaginable sorrow,
the sorrow of lonely creatures calling out from
    distant universes,
to move through you, to penetrate to your very core.

And prepare for joys so unbearable
you'll wonder why your heart hasn't exploded yet.

Prepare for love to drain your tear ducts.
Prepare to fall on your knees time and time again,
in awe, in horror, in gratitude, in the deepest calm.
Prepare to never be prepared again.

If you want to "feel good" all the time,
if you want pleasure without pain, joy without sorrow,
light without night; if you want a "feel good" spirituality,
please, I beg you:

Turn back.
Turn back, right now!

171 Dying to Live

Don't wait until you are dying.
You are dying.
So live.

Live this day, this precious day, this immediate day, so
    pregnant with potential, so saturated with wonder.
Tomorrow is a wish, a promise, a hope, a longing,
    an expectation, a happy dream.

Yesterday served its purpose well.
Today is all that is left.
Today is everything.
Feel life pumping through your veins today.
Risk. Speak out. Forget there was ever such a thing
    as normality.
Be unexpected. Make a mess. Ruin your image.
Laugh at the idea of a fixed "self."
Sacrifice your certainty on the altar of aliveness.

Be here, on this day.
Cherish its pains and its joys.
It is yours, forever.

Your Life Cannot Go Wrong

In reality, your world is set up so that nothing happens *to* you, but everything happens *for* you—for your awakening, for your growth, for your inspiration, for your exploration—even if you forget that, or sometimes cannot see it, or sometimes fall into distraction and despair.

When there is no fixed destination, you cannot ever lose your destination, so you cannot ever lose your path, so nothing that happens in your life can take you off your path. Your path *is* what happens, and what happens *is* your path. There is no other.

Everything is a gift on this unbreakable path that you call your life—the laughter, the tears, the times of great sorrow, the experiences of profound loss, the pain, the confusion, the times you believe you'll never make it, even the overwhelming heartbreak of love—even if you forget that sometimes, or cannot see that sometimes, or absolutely lose faith in the entire show sometimes.

But even the loss of faith in the show is part of the show, and even the scene where "something goes wrong" is not indicative of the show going wrong, and so you are always exactly where you need to be, believe it or not, even if you are not.

Life can be trusted absolutely, even when trust seems a million light years away, and life cannot go wrong, for all is life, and life is all. Understand this, know it in your heart: spirituality is profoundly simple, as simple as breathing, as natural as gazing up at the stars at night and falling into silent wonder.

The universe is more beautiful than you could ever imagine.

173 The Pathless Path

Don't view a thought or a feeling, however "negative" or intense, as a block to your path. See it as an ally, a friend, a welcome guide along the path. An unexpected visitor, a fellow traveler.

Because the path has no fixed destination, there is no "correct" version of the present moment. Any moment, however uncomfortable, is nothing less than a brilliant manifestation of your path, which leads you not away from where you are, but liberates you from the exhausting urge to be anywhere else. The path has no path but itself, no destination except the thrilling journey, and no moment is a mistake along it.

It's a falling in love with where you are, with the present step. And here, there are only guides, allies, gatekeepers, and friends. New ways to see, ingenious ways to remember.

Challenges, yes. But a willingness to face whatever shows up along the way.

The one thing that will never abandon you, friend, is the one thing you have always sought.

174 Your Life, Inhabited

Dedicate your life to love today, for death is near. This is not depressing, this is the Way, this has always been the Way.

Death comes to all of us, the saint and the sinner alike, the rich and the poor, the amoeba and the Milky Way; she comes in the night or in the brilliant light of day; she comes unexpectedly, often without warning; she has no use for your plans, your dreams of what might be. She is ruthlessly unsentimental, honest, a free spirit, a lover—and hopelessly misunderstood.

She will switch off the movie in the middle of any scene, any scene at all. She does not discriminate. The great love scene, the scene of unbearable ecstasy, the scene where everything is at last working out, the scene of great success and adulation, the scene in which death seems so distant, she will come in the middle of the scene, and she will whisper in your ear, "This is it. . . . Let go . . ."

Without her, life would lose all its meaning, for meaning is made only in relation to or from death and finitude and boundedness. Infinite nothing cannot mean anything to infinite nothing. Awareness has no meaning unto itself. Death grounds us in life's rhythms.

If we lived forever, we would come to take everything for granted. Every encounter with a friend or lover would lose its preciousness. We would have infinite time to make amends, to heal, to serve, to learn, to give what we have to give. There would be no need or desire to touch our grief, our deepest longings, meet our wounds. We could put it all off for ten thousand years. The words we longed to speak today, the truth we longed to tell, we could abandon indefinitely, and it wouldn't matter. Our days would lose their bittersweet urgency. We would disconnect from the mystery of our hearts. The ego, with its fears, would reign supreme.

Infinite time, existence without death, yin without yang, would render life in many ways unlivable, the movie unwatchable, the story deathly dull or too horrible to contemplate. We would lose ourselves in the contemplation of the real possibility of pain without end, sorrows without cessation, no way out.

For many, the thought of the end actually makes the day bearable, brings relief. The knowledge of our impermanence can even invite a sweetness into our days, and can help us connect with gratitude, that wonderful balm without which life is cold and empty.

Finitude is not the enemy. The body and its limitations, its secretions and boundaries are not our own, yet they are teachers of grace, too.

Finitude within infinity. Boundaries dancing in unboundedness. An equation that the human mind has never been able to solve. And never needs to.

Death is coming, so dedicate your life now to that which never dies—love, compassion, and a gentle presence. Expand into the vastness of love; take a universe into your heart. Turn toward the moment; attention makes it sacred.

And as the movie switches off, perhaps you will remember that whether you loved or hated the movie, it was a gift. And then, loved or hated, the entire movie itself will be reduced to a single memory, and that single thought-form will disappear into nothingness, and the nothingness will disappear . . .

Oh. Did anything happen at all? Is this a death, or a birth? Falling into unknowing. Undivided from the mystery. Back to the great Womb from which you were never separate, released from the ravages of time . . .

You loved, friend, and you walked your path, and sometimes you stumbled, and you didn't resolve everything you expected to resolve before the end. There are tasks left undone, questions left unanswered, words that were never spoken, final scenes left unseen. But perhaps total resolution was the lie, and your days were only there to be savored, not wrapped up neatly.

Focus on what was given, not on what was taken away, nor on what will never be.

You loved, you tried, you did more than your best, you touched others and were touched deeply in return, you inhabited your days, the days that were given, you laughed and you cried, and none of it is any less meaningful now because it is ending.

The light of attention is brighter now, the curiosity stronger, the presence warmer, the intimacy deeper. It was only ever about the journey, friend, it was never about reaching the destination, getting to the finish line. You are too courageous for destinations, too alive for resolution.

The meaning of your life is your life, inhabited.

There Are No Endings

There is nothing more glorious than the beginning of
the path. Your heart soaring with possibility, you take
that first baby step into the unknown. Trembling but
alive, you walk.

It was never about getting to the end, reaching
the finish line; it was always about falling in love
with the beginnings. And life is always a beginning.
Each step, each breath, each brand new day, each
invitation to surrender, each sunset, each dawn,
each wave of joy or sorrow, each chance to trust.

The ocean's waves do not end, they only fall back
into their ocean, their Source, emerging again, falling,
playing like children of infinity, held in unspeakable
love. From the perspective of the Source, nothing
has happened at all, except the dance. Endings are
beginnings, and beginnings are endings, here in the
vastness of presence.

At the intersection, we meet. I don't know you,
and you don't know me. Brought together by destiny
or chance, we dance in the ocean's depths.

If you ran out of oxygen, I would breathe you.

176 Your New Path

You do not know exactly where you are going, and you cannot go back to the place from which you came. It is perfectly natural to feel afraid, and fear only needs to be felt anyway. In every Now, a billion possible futures are born and die, a billion possible lives are lived to completion or not, and you walk here at the Origin. Stay close to life at the place where it happens. Look back only to celebrate your innocence.

You can expect to feel groundless sometimes, for everything will be falling into uncertainty as you walk. Do not resist the urge to know, but do not seek your sanctuary there either. For there is actual safety in falling; you can only fall more deeply into yourself.

Some may call this journey a risk, but the only true risk is to live in complacency. The only true pain is the unwillingness to feel it. You will lose the old securities, but you will soon discover that they were never, ever real.

Tired of the lies, nauseated by the easy answers, you will watch in astonishment as the old path crumbles, and a brilliant new path forges itself with every step. Your only guide now is the heart, and the breaths, and the sound of your own life (closer now), and a wisdom forged in glorious doubt.

Your heart may be pounding, your legs may be trembling, you may feel more insecure than ever, but you are alive, my love, you are alive.

Why You Cannot Fail

You cannot fail.

You can fall to your knees sometimes, yes, you can find yourself standing in the rubble of shattered dreams, dreams that seemed so real yesterday when you were younger than today and full of hope and had time to dream and everything seemed so certain, like a childhood so rich in light and color and beginnings that its ending seemed so far away, yet it ended.

And you cry out, "Old Life, where have you gone, why have you forsaken me, where did I go wrong?" But you cannot fail.

You can walk or not walk down a path you know or do not, turn back, lose your way, wonder where you went wrong, lose the map and lose the others and lose yourself in the wondering, you can stumble and fall in the darkness, but you cannot fail.

You can lose the future, or at least lose the dream of the future, or at least lose the hope of a dream of a tomorrow that may or may not happen, lose yesterday's dreams of tomorrows which look nothing like today, but you cannot fail.

You can stop, take a breath, feel the heart thumping in your chest, feel the surge of life in your body, life surging as a broken heart, disappointment, despair, or some other ancient longing that you have never been able to name, let alone satisfy, feel as open and as vulnerable and as devoid of answers as you did when you were a little baby overwhelmed by the uncontrollable cacophony of existence, not knowing if the next step forward would take you back, or a step back would take you forward, but you cannot fail.

You can fall to the ground, exhausted and fed up today with the push and the pull of chance and chaos, with the decisions and pressures and expectations that never seem to end, the sound and the fury of being a person in a world that moves so fast, and you feel so slow, and you can feel yourself on the ground, and you can feel the ground holding you up, and you can feel its solidity, the way it supports you without ever asking, but you cannot fail.

You cannot fail because you are taking a breath now, you have been given another breath, your heart is beating away, and you know you are alive. And you don't know much else, and you don't know what the next step will be, but perhaps, somewhere deep in your bones, there is an inkling of the step you have to take now, and perhaps that is the step of taking no step at all, taking the step of feeling your breath at last, feeling your belly rise and fall at last, on this new day of your new life, feeling your tired feet planted firmly on the ground at last, a new and more stable earth that is still emerging from the fertilizer of the old earth and of your ancestors buried there, a ground that holds you up, that allows you to breathe, and stand, or not stand, or fall, or wonder what the future may hold, because it has all been thrown into uncertainty now, thrown back into the chaos whence it came. But you cannot fail.

An old way of life has fallen away, but you cannot fail. A way of life that was no longer working for you, you had outgrown, that is too small for you now, that would limit the vastness that you are; that is what has failed, withered, died, returned to the fertile ground. But you have not failed. An old identity, a role has disappeared, a character you were playing you have stopped playing, an outdated script from an outdated movie has been taken from you, words that were never your own words anyway, words that you spoke yesterday, but you never really meant yesterday because you knew perhaps in your very cells that tomorrow was coming and would bring with it truth, and realness, and would break you open in ways you never imagined. But you cannot fail. The forms have shifted, the roles have changed, old identities have dissolved into a greater one, that's all, one that contains more possibility and life and creativity than you could ever imagine, but you cannot fail.

You cannot fail because you are alive, and you breathe the breath of a sparkling cosmos, each in-breath a victory, each out-breath a celebration, not of you as you were going to be, but of you as you actually are. You cannot fail because you are present now to your heart, your heart that was for so long neglected, you have been forced into contact with your heart, and all the successes in the world could never have given you the gift that you are being given now. The gift of failing and turning toward that failure, the possibility of coming close to yourself, of holding yourself and not waiting any longer to be held, of breathing in and out and not missing the miracle of it, of feeling the belly rising and falling and no longer taking it for granted. Of feeling the most primitive feelings full of wisdom surging through your body and no longer running away from them into some future you only half believed in anyway.

You have not failed because you have finally arrived. You have not failed because you have remembered yourself again, here, remembered the gift that you forgot because you were so afraid to fail. The worst has already happened, so you can rest now in this emerging world.

There is no failure except in the abandonment of yourself, in the ignoring of the preciousness of each and every moment. You can feel like a failure, yes, you can cry and scream and curse God and the universe and fate and karma and the alignment of the planets and all that, but you cannot fail. For even your tears, your cries, your deepest guttural wails are holy, and held by life; and the fact that you are in contact with yourself now, no longer numb but alive to your numbness, awake to your pain and your joy, is a sign that you are, at last, on the right path.

And the path that you thought was the right path, the right path that turned out to be the wrong path, because it led to failure, was the right path after all, because your failure has been your portal, and so you have not failed, and there is no right path, no wrong path, only the path that you walk.

And it all fades into memory anyway, and into night, and you know now to keep yourself close. Any path you walk will only lead you here. You may take the wrong path again, and dream again of failure, and then you will wake up, and breathe, and contact the preciousness of another moment on this strange and beautiful planet spinning on its axis, and you will know again, you are on the path. The path ended and began only with you, and beyond success and failure; you are awake now, and asking questions you never would have asked before, and coming closer to what really matters, and feeling things you spent a lifetime trying to avoid, and it's not so bad after all. Thinking about failure is a thousand times worse than living it. And you only have to live a moment of it.

And what once seemed like a nightmare is not a nightmare. It is just the next breath, and the next thud of the heart, and these sensations dancing in the belly, chest, and throat, and the sound of the bird as he sings before sleep, and the evening breeze, and the cat cuddling up to your feet, and that ancient feeling of being broken but alive, broken but so damn alive, and unbroken still.

And willing to be here. Having the courage to be here, despite history, despite what may or may not happen as you walk down untrodden paths to new futures. You will take this moment, imperfect as it is, over no moment at all. You will take this life, this failure, this success, this joy, this pain, this courage, this mystery, this great story unfolding, and you will love it; you will love it even when you find it hard to love it, even when you cannot love it. You will love that, you will love your inability to love it sometimes.

You cannot fail because you cannot be defined, you cannot be contained, you cannot be something that you are not. And you are life, you are every sacred breath, you are that sense of wonder you had when you were a child and hadn't yet learned about failure, you are adventure, and the willingness to fall and get up again, to fall again, to get up again, to fall. To get up, and to brush yourself off, and to stand tall, because there is dignity in falling after

all, and dignity in admitting you are not finished,
in reminding yourself that you are not in control of
everything that happens, and that sometimes you
need to learn a little humility again, as if you didn't
already know.

Your story is not yet complete. All great heroes fall
and doubt themselves, and often stand on the verge
of giving up. Courage is not brute strength nor the
absence of fear but the willingness to feel like a little
baby again, to doubt everything, and then to stand
anyway, to give up and to stand anyway, Fail, fall,
rest. Keep resting. And stand. And breathe. And out
of the ashes will emerge a new "yes!" to life, more
powerful than ever before because you have absorbed
all the power of what they called your failure.

But what do they know of your courage?

And perhaps you will fail again, and again, but
you don't care anymore, you are willing to fail, to
succeed at failing, because you know deep down that
you cannot fail. Life is now an adventure, not the
attempt to never fail, nor the desperation to succeed,
but the chance to love yourself here, hold yourself
so close as you finally walk the path of your heart,
perhaps more fearlessly now than ever before, more
trusting of the occasional devastation, the inevitable
wrong turns that turn out to be the right ones for
your path.

You have not lost your path but found it. You have not lost your heart but come closer to it. You have not conquered fear but finally befriended it. You have not failed. You cannot fail. Your heart has never heard of failure anyway. This human language was always too small for you.

The dinosaurs did not fail. They lived, and until the fire came, they savored every moment. And those last few dinosaurs, looking up into the burning sky, perhaps just looked up in wonder. Thank you for having given me life. Thank you for having given me life.

And behold, a new Earth.

About the Author

Jeff Foster studied astrophysics at Cambridge University. In his mid-twenties, after a long period of depression and illness, he became addicted to the idea of "spiritual enlightenment" and embarked on an intensive spiritual quest for the ultimate truth of existence.

The spiritual search came crashing down with the clear recognition of the non-dual nature of everything and the discovery of the extraordinary in the ordinary. In the clarity of this seeing, life became what it always was: intimate, open, loving, and spontaneous, and Jeff was left with a deep understanding of the root illusion behind human suffering and a love of the present moment.

Jeff presently holds meetings, retreats, and private one-on-one sessions around the world.

Visit him online at lifewithoutacentre.com.

About Sounds True

Sounds True is a multimedia publisher whose mission is to inspire and support personal transformation and spiritual awakening. Founded in 1985 and located in Boulder, Colorado, we work with many of the leading spiritual teachers, thinkers, healers, and visionary artists of our time. We strive with every title to preserve the essential "living wisdom" of the author or artist. It is our goal to create products that not only provide information to a reader or listener, but that also embody the quality of a wisdom transmission.

For those seeking genuine transformation, Sounds True is your trusted partner. At SoundsTrue.com you will find a wealth of free resources to support your journey, including exclusive weekly audio interviews, free downloads, interactive learning tools, and other special savings on all our titles.

To learn more, please visit SoundsTrue.com/freegifts or call us toll-free at 800.333.9185.